Would You Lend Your Toothbrush?

HEATHER BRAZIER

with illustrations by Kate Parkinson

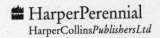
W9-CIB-552

HarperPerennial
HarperCollinsPublishersLtd

Illustrations copyright © 1995 by Kate Parkinson

First edition: 1995

Canadian Cataloguing in Publication Data

Brazier, Heather, 1962–
Would you lend your toothbrush? : more of what Canadians borrow, eat,
watch, buy and do– on an average day

ISBN 0-00-638054-9

1. Canada — Miscellanea.   2. Canada — Statistics.   I. Title.

FC61.B73 1995   971.064'8'02   C95-930439-8
F1008.3.B73 1995

---

95 96 97 98 99 ❖ HC 10 9 8 7 6 5 4 3 2 1

Printed and bound in the United States

For Frederick John, my dear dad,
with love from your little girl

average n. 1. the typical or normal amount, quality, degree, etc.
2. the result obtained by adding the numbers or quantities in a set and dividing the total by the number of members in the set. Also called: arithmetic mean.

The Collins English Dictionary

Contents

Acknowledgements

Typically, there is only one name that is attached to a book and that is its author's. In reality, there are many people that deserve recognition for the invaluable guidance, talent, advice and support given.

To Susan Broadhurst, your editorial expertise, guidance and patience, combined with a wonderful sense of humour, are the reasons this book was such a pleasure to create.

To Kate Parkinson, my talented illustrator, your drawings bring humour and animation to my text.

To Rebecca Vogan, your eagle eye and adeptness with your copy editor's pencil, as well as an abundance of yellow sticky notes, put my manuscript in polished form.

To my extended family of aunts, uncles and dozens of cousins, you have always shown me nothing but love and support through good times, bad times and everything in between.

To my ever growing circle of friends, you are the ones who share in my laughter and tears. Each of you plays an irreplaceable role in my life.

And, finally, to HarperCollins Publishers Ltd, thank you for believing in me.

Introduction

What is an average day in Canada? That question has over 28 million answers. Each of us goes through the same 24-hour day, yet no two of us spend our time in exactly the same way. For that reason, there is an unlimited supply of pieces that can be put together in what could be described as a never-finished jigsaw puzzle.

As was stated in *Which Do You Prefer: Chunky or Smooth?*, the outside edge of this puzzle represents Canada. The inside pieces are Canadians themselves and the things we do on an average day.

The numerical values used in this book most often come from annual figures. Consequently, one must divide the annual amount by 365 to obtain a daily statistic. It must be assumed, for the purposes of this book, that each of these events occurs each and every day. The exceptions to this "rule" are prefaced with statements such as "On an average Mother's Day...", "On an average Father's Day..." or "On an average summer day..."

Compiling this book allowed your intrepid gatherer to continue the adventure into the wise and wacky world of facts and figures. Here's to many more adventures along this unique Canadian superhighway of life.

Heather Brazier
April 1995

Would You Lend Your Toothbrush?

PEOPLE AND PETS

on an average day...

Baby face...

... It costs $160,741 to raise a child from birth to age 18 in an average Canadian two-parent family with both parents working. That works out to $24.47 for each of 6,570 days

... During a child's first seven months, new parents spend $9.52 on baby products. Drugstores sell 50% of all disposable diapers purchased across the country and 60% of all infant formula

... 500,000 children aged 13 and under are cared for by a relative (usually a grandmother) while the child's parents are at work

on an average day...

... Day-care costs for a 3-year-old child placed in for-profit day-care centres across the country are:

$26.80 in Toronto
$26.40 in Ottawa
$25.80 in Yellowknife
$23.00 in London
$22.40 in Whitehorse
$21.20 in Winnipeg
$20.40 in Quebec City
$19.60 in Halifax
$18.80 in Vancouver
$18.60 in Saskatoon
$18.40 in Montreal
$17.60 in Calgary
$17.00 in Victoria
$16.60 in Edmonton
$16.60 in St. John's
$16.40 in Regina
$14.00 in Saint John

... It costs $87 to rent a camouflage video-surveillance system called Babywatch to monitor the baby-sitter or nanny while the baby's parents are out of the house

on an average day...

... 20% of 5-year-old children wet their beds, 7% of 7 year olds do likewise and 2% of teenagers are bedwetters

... Most popular baby names in Canada, 1950–1990

1950		1970		1990	
Boys	Girls	Boy	Girls	Boys	Girls
Robert	Linda	Michael	Lisa	Michael	Jessica
David	Patricia	David	Michelle	Matthew	Amanda
John	Barbara	Robert	Jennifer	Christopher	Sarah
James	Susan	Jason	Tracy	Andrew	Stephanie
William	Sharon	James	Tammy	Kyle	Samantha
Richard	Margaret	Christopher	Karen	Ryan	Ashley
Kenneth	Donna	John	Nicole	Joshua	Brittany
Donald	Judith	Richard	Christine	Daniel	Jennifer
Ronald	Carol	Kevin	Shannon	Jordan	Nicole
Douglas	Sandra	Mark	Susan	Justin	Kayla

... The most popular names for girls born in British Columbia are Ashley, Megan, Brittany and Jessica
... The most popular names for boys born in British Columbia are Brandon, Kyle, Ryan and Jordan

WOULD YOU LEND YOUR TOOTHBRUSH?

on an average day...

... The most popular names for girls born in Ontario are Jessica, Sarah, Samantha and Stephanie
... The most popular names for boys born in Ontario are Michael, Matthew, Christopher and Andrew

Primary concerns...

... 85 children need medical care at a hospital due to accidents in and around their home

Of the total,

31 suffer falls
22 are injured playing sports
4 are hurt on playground equipment
4 are treated for poisoning
3 are burned or scalded
21 are "other accidents"

on an average day...

... The Regional Poison Information Centre, located in Toronto's Hospital for Sick Children, logs 93 calls relating to children under the age of 6 who have swallowed medications, chemicals or cleaners. The top 10 most common poisons ingested by children:

household cleaning products
plants
children's analgesics
cough and cold preparations
bleaches
antihistamines
insecticides
mercury from thermometers
perfumes
children's vitamins

... 11 children are injured in automobile accidents
... Less than 50% of riders under the age of 6 are properly buckled up in safety restraints
... Every fifth day a child is killed in a car accident

on an average day...

... 2 children end up in emergency rooms due to mishaps on in-line skates

... 3 child abductions take place; 2 of these children are taken by a parent or guardian

... 167 cases of missing children are reported across the country

Of the total,

96 of these children are female
71 are male

123 are classed as runaways who voluntarily left home

on an average day...

... 115 children under the age of 15 are sexually abused by an adult

... 2,500,000 Canadians watched the debut of the two-part television drama, *The Boys of St. Vincent*, broadcast nationally in December 1993. During the broadcast, more than a thousand calls were made to Kids Help Phone crisis lines by middle-aged men recalling similar abuse from 20 to 30 years ago

... 4 in 10 children witness violence in their parents' marriage

on an average day...

Child behaviour...

... When Canadians are asked how the behaviour of
young people today compares to the behaviour of
young people a decade ago:

2% say it's much better today
5% say it's somewhat better today
17% say it's about the same
31% say it's somewhat worse
45% say it's much worse

Teen scene...

... In many single-parent families, up to 35% of the
household duties are done by the children, including
cooking, cleaning, shopping and laundry

on an average day...

... According to a national survey of Canadian teenagers:

> 60% expect to graduate from university
> 75% expect to be more financially comfortable than their parents
> 95% expect to own a home
> 90% say they have a right to the kind of employment their education has prepared them for
> 41% think job advancement will involve working overtime
> 43% believe the national debt will be paid off in their lifetime

... 86% of teens expect to marry for life
... 84% of teens expect to have children
... 10% of teens approve of sex outside of marriage

... Canada's suicide rate for youths aged 15 to 24 is the third highest in the world. Australia has the highest rate, followed by Norway

on an average day...

... With 345 beds in nine youth hostels, Metropolitan Toronto has more beds available than the rest of Canada combined

... 94% of female high school students are victims of sexual harassment from their male peers. They are subjected to everything from lewd comments to inappropriate touching

... 56 Ontario teens call 1-800-INFO-SEX, Planned Parenthood of Ontario's Facts of Life line

... More teenagers lose their virginity in June than in any other month of the year

on an average day...

... 35% of young people aged 12 to 17 are the primary consumers of pornography and express interest in watching sexually violent scenes involving rape, torture and bondage

... When teens are asked what their most cherished items of clothing are, they reply jeans, athletic wear and Doc Marten shoes

... 500 pairs of Doc Martens are sold in Canada

on an average day...

... Approximately 500 students in Toronto use counterfeit Toronto Transit Commission tickets, which they make themselves

Fun for all...

...Preschool toys account for 20% of all toys sold in Canada

... Whitman Golden publishes 2 of its very popular "Little Golden Books"

on an average day...

... As part of its continuing effort to reduce illiteracy, Whitman Golden donates 205 of its books to reading programs and organizations

... The Barbie doll, on the Canadian market for 32 years, garners 85% of the fashion doll market

... Canadians buy $123,288 worth of Super Mario games

... Of the 25,000 Canadian kids aged 6 to 16 who compete in the annual Chess Challenge, run by Larry Bevand of Chess 'n' Math, 98% are male

on an average day...

Femme facts...

...There are 220,000 Girl Guides in Canada, belonging to more than 13,000 packs; 45,000 Canadian women volunteer as Guide leaders

... 52% of the total full-time students enrolled at the University of Toronto are women. In 1884, the university admitted its first 10 female students

... 11% of Canadian architects are female

... 25% of all lawyers practising in Canada are female

on an average day...

... The TTC, Canada's largest public transit system, employs 1,227 women, of whom 346 are vehicle operators

... The average diamond engagement ring retails for $1,760

Interestingly:

89% of first-time brides receive a diamond ring
Most engagement rings are purchased between the beginning of October and the end of December
Round diamonds are the favourite, followed by pear shaped

... 94% of grooms receive a wedding band from their brides; 36% of these rings have at least one diamond

... 312,000 men paying alimony and child support spend $4,109,589 or $13.17 each
... There are 90,000 unpaid support orders representing $1,287,671 in delinquent payments
... Only 2% of those receiving alimony are men

on an average day...

... 1 woman dies in childbirth every 44 days. This figure compares to 4 deaths a day between 1921 and 1930, when the Canadian population was one third what it is today

... 1 woman is killed by her partner every three days

Womenspeak...

... If housework were a paying proposition, stay-at-home mothers would be paid $45, according to Statistics Canada. The average cost of hiring someone to do the housework in a home with one preschool child would be $72

on an average day...

... 74% of women in two-parent households with children under age 19 say they do more cleaning and laundry than their husbands do

... 79% of women surveyed say they do not trust their husbands to do the laundry

... 77% of women say they are the prime influence on what car is chosen for the household

... 67% of women say that car salesmen do not take them seriously, especially if they visit the showroom with a man

on an average day...

... 47% of Canadian women would not choose their current partner as their perfect date
... 70% of Canadians think it is okay for a woman to ask a man for a date
... 60% of women who ask a man out insist on paying for the date
... 93% of women say they absolutely do not want a man ordering for them in a restaurant
... 42% of women say the best place to meet men is at work or school
... 14% say bars and restaurants are the best place
... 8% choose health clubs

... When 5,000 women in 14 countries were asked by Harlequin Enterprises to rank the world's sexiest men, Greek men placed 1st, Canadian men ranked 5th and American men rated 7th

on an average day...

Looking for love?...

... The best cities in which to find a potential husband are:

Thompson, Manitoba
Fort McMurray, Alberta
Grand Centre, Alberta
Labrador City, Newfoundland
Kitimat, British Columbia

... The best cities in which to find a potential wife are:

Cobourg, Ontario
Tillsonburg, Ontario
Lindsay, Ontario
Yorkton, Saskatchewan
Camrose, Alberta
St. Hyacinthe, Quebec

Buying beauty...

... Canadians spend $4,416,712 in the country's 16,161 beauty parlours and barber shops

on an average day...

... Men spend 19 minutes primping; women spend 23.5 minutes doing the same

... Men spend $931,507 on health and beauty products; women spend $2,465,753 on the same

Seniority...

... 500 Canadians turn 65 years old

... There are 1.3 million men and 1.8 million women who are senior citizens in Canada

on an average day...

... 58 Canadians become members of the Canadian Association for Retired Persons

Mature money...

... Canadian seniors spend $54,794,520 on goods and services

... Canadian seniors pay $15,890,410 in income taxes

Elder care...

... 7% of people aged 65 and over are in long-term institutional care. This figure rises to 33% for Canadians aged 85 and over

on an average day...

... People over age 64 represent 12% of the population in Canada, yet they take 30% of all medications prescribed

... 15% of these seniors take more than one prescription drug

... 3% of children have daily contact with grandparents

... Sources of emotional support for elderly men and women without spouses:

	For Men	For Women
Daughter	16%	28%
Son	7%	12%
Sibling	7%	9%
Other relative	6%	5%
Friend	24%	16%
No one	9%	7%
Neighbour, clergy, doctor, etc.	31%	23%

on an average day...

Parting words...

... Canadians spend $2,209,315 for funeral services

... 20 Canadians have chosen cryonics to put death on hold. Upon dying, their bodies will be placed in liquid nitrogen in the hope that one day the disease that took their life will be curable and their bodies can be "unfrozen." This procedure is available only in the United States

... The federal government pays out $521,918 in death benefits to the families of deceased people. The amount paid, intended to help with funeral expenses, is based on the income of the deceased; the average benefit is $2,310

on an average day...

... Smith Monument Co. Ltd., one of the oldest such companies in Canada, uses 3,300 kilograms of granite to produce 5 headstones and monuments

... 6 graves are dug in Mount Pleasant Cemetery in Toronto, one of Canada's oldest graveyards. It takes 20 minutes to dig a grave in the summer and 40 minutes in the winter

... Halifax's Old Burying Ground is Canada's only graveyard designated as a historical site

on an average day...

Doggie data...

... The 10 most popular dog breeds in Canada:

German Shepherd
Labrador Retriever
Golden Retriever
Shetland Sheepdog
Rottweiler
Poodle
American Cocker Spaniel
Shih Tzu
Miniature Schnauzer
Yorkshire Terrier

... 68 puppies are shipped from the United States for sale in Canadian pet shops
... We spend $32,877 buying American-bred puppies

on an average day...

... The calorie intake for Canadian dogs is as follows:

Dog's Weight (kg.)	Calories
4.5	285–475
9	475–680
13.5	650–930
18	800–1,150
22.5	950–1,360
27	1,090–1,560
36.5	1,360–1,940
45.5	1,605–2,290

... Toronto's animal control officers respond to 6 complaints of dogs-at-large and 7 requests to remove a variety of dead animals from city streets and public areas

on an average day...

Pet ills, vet bills...

... To take a dog or a cat to the vet for an office visit costs $20–$40; the human equivalent would cost $25

... A single vaccination for a dog or cat costs $15; for humans, $8

... To neuter a dog or cat costs $35–$100; a man would pay $700–$750 for a vasectomy

... To spay a dog or cat costs $50–$150; a woman would pay $1,000–$2,000 for a tubal ligation

... Cataract surgery on both eyes of a dog or cat costs $1,000–$1,200; for humans, the cost would be $3,400

... 6 weeks worth of chemotherapy on a dog or cat costs $1,000–$2,000; for human cancer patients, the cost would be $3,200–$9,200

... A CAT scan for a dog or cat costs $300; for a human, $200–$300

... An MRI scan of a dog or cat costs $500; for a human scan, the cost is $700–$800

on an average day...

... Premiums for Pet Plan, the only pet health insurance
plan in Canada, range from 33 cents to 83 cents. Pet
Plan, which will insure any dog or cat between 12
weeks and 8 years, covers accidents and sickness but
not regular vaccinations and checkups. Claim pay-
ments range from $60 to $2,500 per accident or illness

OUR BELIEFS

on an average day...

Religious affiliation...

... When Canadians are asked which religious denomination they belong to:

9,270,000 say Roman Catholic
2,521,000 say United
1,892,000 say Anglican
1,746,000 are affiliated with another Protestant group
2,492,000 say no religion
1,851,000 give no answer

Let us sing...

... According to the United Church's survey of the most popular hymns, selected from hymn books of several denominations and from 2,500 other submissions, the top 10 are:

Praise the Lord With the Sound of the Trumpet
Spirit, Spirit of Gentleness
Joyful, Joyful We Adore You
Let All Things Now
Jesus Bids Us Shine

on an average day...

In a Bulb There Is a Flower
All the Way My Saviour Leads Me
All Things Bright and Beautiful
Child of Blessing, Child of Promise
Amazing Grace / What a Friend We Have in Jesus
(tied)

Sistering...

... 30,707 Canadian women are devoting their life to God in 250 religious orders across the country. Of these:

63% are over age 65
50% are over age 75
only 3% are under
age 44

on an average day...

... Every 6 days, a Canadian woman enters a convent to become a religious sister

... Every 4 days, a religious sister decides to leave the order

A significant synagogue...

... 2,800 Conservative Jews belong to Toronto's Beth Tzedec Synagogue, North America's largest Conservative Jewish congregation

Zen...

... 200 Torontonians belong to the Zen Buddhist Temple and 1,300 are on the mailing list; 97% of the members are Caucasian. A total of 163,415 Canadians identify themselves as practicing Buddhists

SCHOOL DAYS

on an average day...

Educational achievement...

... How Canadians rate internationally in terms of education:

	No high school diploma	High school graduate	College degree or higher
United States	17%	47%	36%
Germany	18%	60%	22%
Canada	24%	36%	40%
Britain	35%	49%	16%
Australia	44%	25%	31%
France	49%	35%	16%

A primary glimpse...

... Of the 2,505 teachers in the Toronto public school system, 633 are men

on an average day...

... 27 inquiries are made to the Toronto-based Canadian
Alliance of Homeschoolers from parents interested in
teaching their children at home

Strictly private...

... To enrol a girl in the following private schools would
cost:

	Day Student	Boarder
Miss Edgar's and Miss Cramp's, Westmount	$14.72	
Crofton House, Vancouver	$22.22	
Bishop Strachan, Toronto	$27.40	$54.79
Branksome Hall, Toronto	$28.09	$57.53
Havergal College, Toronto	$28.09	$57.53

... To enrol a boy in the following private schools would
cost:

	Day Student	Boarder
St. George's College, Vancouver	$20.56	$44.88
Upper Canada College, Toronto	$32.27	$58.93
Trinity College, Port Hope	$33.56	$55.62
St. Andrew's College, Aurora	$33.59	$56.25

on an average day...

... To enrol a student in the following co-ed private
   schools would cost:

	Day Student	Boarder
St. John Ravencourt, Winnipeg	$20.68	$40.45
Ridley College, St. Catharines	$38.36	$60.27

A secondary look...

... When Grade 11 students (or equivalent) in different
   countries are given the same math test, the percentage
   of students who score 100% in each country is:

73% in South Korea
71% in Switzerland
64% in France
62% in Canada
55% in the United States

on an average day...

... The percentage of high school students who spend more than two hours each day on their homework is, by country:

55% in France
41% in South Korea
29% in the United States
27% in Canada
20% in Switzerland

... The percentage of high school students who watch five or more hours of television each day is, by country:

20% in the United States
14% in France
11% in South Korea
7% in Switzerland
5% in Canada

... 100,000 high school students are involved in co-operative education programs that allow them to work part-time in businesses affiliated with the school program

on an average day...

... When Canadian high school students are asked, "What is the difference between astronomy and astrology?", 55% do not know

... At the Grade 10 level, 95% of students say they expect to go to university; less than 35% actually will

... 60% of junior and senior high school students carry a weapon

... 34% of full-time high school students have a part-time job during the school year

on an average day...

A higher degree...

... 64% of Canadians aged 20 to 24 are enrolled in full-time educational college and university programs

... 246,000 women and 222,000 men attend full-time undergraduate university programs

... 767 students are approved for loans to pay for their education. They receive a maximum of $23.57 per day

... Ryerson Polytechnic University has the largest anglophone undergraduate business school in Canada, with 12,000 full-time and 40,000 part-time students

on an average day...

... 5 undergraduate students graduate from Memorial University in Newfoundland. It is the largest university east of Montreal

... Another 8 students graduate from Memorial University's Fisheries and Maritime Institute and the province's technical and regional colleges

... 18 students at the University of Calgary seek one-on-one counselling for stress-related problems on campus

... 28,000 of Canada's 37,400 full-time university professors have tenure

on an average day...

Student integrity...

... When university and college students were asked, "If you obtained a copy of an important exam before it was given, what would you do?":

46% would return it without looking at it
32% would look at it briefly and then return it
22% would review it closely and prepare answers for the exam

... The provincial breakdown for those who would review the exam closely is as follows:

12% in British Columbia
10% in Alberta
17% in Saskatchewan
18% in Manitoba
18% in Ontario
38% in Quebec
18% in New Brunswick
11% in Nova Scotia
12% in Prince Edward Island
11% in Newfoundland

on an average day...

Students from afar...

... 16,500 Hong Kong students are enrolled in Canadian colleges and universities

... For $11.67, Fact Finders of Vancouver and Toronto, hired by parents in Hong Kong, will spy on their sons and daughters studying in Canada and report back on their study habits and progress

WORKING WAYS

on an average day...

Our financial position...

... 31% of Canadians believe their financial situation has worsened recently
... 36% believe it has stayed the same
... 33% believe it has improved

... The provincial breakdown for those who believe their financial situation has worsened is as follows:

26% in British Columbia
34% in Alberta
51% in Saskatchewan
30% in Manitoba
27% in Ontario
38% in Quebec
27% in New Brunswick
37% in Nova Scotia
31% in Prince Edward Island
42% in Newfoundland

on an average day...

Incoming facts...

... The average Canadian family income is $140.66

... Metro Toronto has the highest per capita income at
$162.88; close behind are Oshawa, Ottawa, Calgary
and Vancouver. The three cities with the lowest per
capita incomes are Montréal-Nord, Trois-Rivières and
Sherbrooke, all in the province of Quebec

... Individuals with the highest average daily income of
$130 live in West Vancouver

... Individuals with the lowest average daily income of
$50 reside in Montréal-Nord

... Employed Canadian women earn $48.63 and
employed Canadian men earn $81.77. The highest
paid employed women in Canada live in Metro
Toronto, earning $60.50

on an average day...

... The average daily wage for working women in the 1990s
is $49; in the 1940s, their average daily wage was $13
... The average daily wage for working men in the 1990s
is $82; in the 1940s, their average daily wage was $26

... Women hold 72% of the lowest paying jobs in Canada
and 20% of the highest paying jobs

... The average major-league baseball player on a
Canadian team makes $4,384
... The average Canadian nurse earns $104
... The average Canadian gas station attendant makes
$43

on an average day...

... The 10 highest paying jobs and the percentage of men and women employed in them are as follows:

Job	Average Daily Pay	% men	% women
Judges and magistrates	$281	78	22
Physicians and surgeons	$280	77	23
Dentists	$262	89	11
Lawyers and notaries	$211	75	25
Senior managers	$186	81	19
Other managers	$178	75	25
Airline pilots, navigators	$176	95	5
Osteopaths and chiropractors	$175	82	18
Engineers and natural science managers	$174	88	12
University professors	$170	78	22

on an average day...

... The 10 lowest paying jobs and the percentage of men and women employed in them are as follows:

Job	Average Daily Pay	% men	% women
Child-care workers	$37	3	97
Food and beverage servers	$39	22	78
Housekeepers and servants	$40	8	92
Cleaners	$43	13	87
Service station workers	$43	80	20
Bartenders	$44	46	54
Livestock farm workers	$45	64	36
Sewing machine and textile workers	$45	9	91
Non-livestock farm workers	$45	55	45
Crop farm workers	$45	51	49

... Comparing the daily wages of Canadians with workers around the world:

Country	Manufacturing Employee	White Collar Worker	Manager	CEO
Britain	$71	$205	$444	$1,204
Canada	$95	$129	$364	$1,139
France	$82	$171	$522	$1,314
Germany	$101	$164	$399	$1,071
Italy	$86	$160	$602	$1,269
Japan	$94	$112	$508	$1,070
United States	$76	$158	$437	$1,965

on an average day...

Career moves...

... Some of the jobs created daily in Canada are:

> 151 in manufacturing
> 142 in construction
> 107 in retail
> 99 in computing industries
> 90 in hotel, restaurant and entertainment services

... Some of the jobs eliminated daily in Canada are:

> 74 in agriculture
> 71 in health services
> 68 in public administration
> 55 in real estate
> 27 in chemical manufacturing

on an average day...

... The 10 fastest-growing jobs in Canada are:

respiratory technicians
systems analysts
dental hygienists
child-care workers
occupational therapists
speech therapists
physiotherapists
data processing operators
claims adjusters
paralegals

... The 10 fastest-growing jobs in the United States are:

home health aides
computer scientists
systems analysts
physiotherapists
paralegals
teachers, special education
medical assistants
corrections officers
child-care workers
travel agents

on an average day...

... The worst career opportunities in Canada are:

fish canners
commercial fishers
railway workers
sewing machine operators
airline pilots
textile weavers
typists
tobacco processors

... The worst career opportunities in the United States
are:

railway workers
directory assistance operators
shoe sewing machine operators
child-care workers, private
job printers
roustabouts
domestic help, private household
motion picture projectionists

on an average day...

... The best places to find a job in Canada are:

Medicine Hat, Alberta
Kingston, Ontario
London, Ontario
Brandon, Manitoba
Rimouski, Quebec

... The worst places to find a job in Canada are:

New Glasgow, Nova Scotia
Sydney Mines, Nova Scotia
Sydney, Nova Scotia
Chatham/Newcastle, New Brunswick
Sept-Iles, Quebec

Danger pay...

... 1,426 Canadians are injured on the job

... The safest job, as assessed by the Workers'
Compensation Board, is accounting

on an average day...

... The 10 most dangerous jobs, as assessed by the Workers' Compensation Board, are:

stevedores (the people who unload boats in port)
mining contractors
wreckers
steel erection workers
tree surgeons
woods operators
diamond drillers
sewer workers
nickel miners
gold miners

on an average day...

In the workplace...

... 360,000 Canadians hold two jobs

... 3 million Canadians work shifts

... 1 million Canadians work on Saturdays
... 500,000 Canadians work on Sundays

... 136,000 Canadians working in 9,000 companies participate in work-sharing programs

... British Columbia generates 2 out of 3 new full-time
jobs in Canada

on an average day...

... Only 23% of Canadian companies have an established policy dealing with sexual harassment in the workplace. Saskatchewan has the best record, with 33% of all companies having such a policy; British Columbia has the worst record, with only 18% of companies having such a policy

... The equivalent of 1,559 days of work are lost to work stoppages and strikes; among 19 countries, Canada is second only to Italy for lost days per 1,000 employees

... 71,429 full-time workers take the day off work for personal reasons. Their absence costs the economy $27,397,260, making it the biggest human resource problem for employers

on an average day...

... 2 million Canadians are subject to on-the-job electronic surveillance to monitor their work habits

... 39% of all middle and upper management jobs are held by women

... When men are asked how opportunities for women to move into senior positions have changed over the past decade:

3% say the opportunity has worsened
12% say it has remained the same
85% say it has improved

... When women are asked the same question:

5% say the opportunity has worsened
19% say it has remained the same
76% say it has improved

on an average day...

... Canada's best employers for women are:

American Express
Bank of Montreal
Canadian Satellite Communications Inc.
City of Toronto
Credit Valley Hospital (Mississauga)
Mount Sinai Hospital (Toronto)
North York Board of Education
St. Elizabeth Visiting Nurses Association of Ontario
Tory Tory DesLauriers & Binnington
Vancouver City Savings Credit Union

CBC...

... A musician performing a
piece of music less than 30
minutes long for the CBC
will be paid $131.10 for a three-
hour "call." If the musician is
unfamiliar with the piece, he or she is
given $33 an hour to learn it

on an average day...

... When the CBC records an orchestra as a part of its regular season, each player receives $152.52 for up to 135 minutes of music

... An actor with a principal part in a CBC radio one-hour drama receives $249.95 for four hours of work

... A guest host on the CBC receives $33.34 per hour for a 45-hour week (in the case of Stereo Morning, that week begins every day at 4:00 a.m.)

... A one-hour *Ideas* documentary on CBC radio, which can involve at least four weeks of conceptualizing, reading, interviewing, and studio work, will net its creator $2,436

Creative employment...

... 500 copies of *Spare Change*, a monthly newspaper produced and sold by unemployed men and women of Vancouver's east side, are sold on street corners for pocket change. Toronto has a similar paper named *The Outrider*

on an average day...

Domestic bliss?...

... 21 new domestic workers are accepted into Canada

Thoughts of retirement...

... When Canadians are asked why they are retiring:

28% have reached the mandatory retirement age of 65
25% are retiring for health reasons
6% are taking early retirement incentive packages
4% have lost their jobs to new technology
37% are retiring for other reasons, such as family
responsibilities or personal choice

... 14% of men over age 60 must continue to work
because of financial reasons
... 11% of women over age 60 must continue to work for
financial reasons

BETTER HOMES
AND GARDENS

on an average day...

The state of real estate...

... There are 423 new housing starts in Canada. The provincial breakdown is as follows:

108 in British Columbia
48 in Alberta
6 in Saskatchewan
9 in Manitoba
128 in Ontario
94 in Quebec
9 in New Brunswick
13 in Nova Scotia
2 in Prince Edward Island
6 in Newfoundland

... An average new house across the country costs:

$247,000 in Vancouver
$110,000 in Edmonton
$130,000 in Calgary
$71,500 in Regina
$75,500 in Saskatoon
$82,000 in Winnipeg
$151,300 in Hamilton

on an average day...

$215,500 in Toronto
$144,000 in Ottawa
$112,450 in Montreal
$103,170 in Halifax

... The average homeowner pays $22.73 per day in mortgage payments
... The average renter pays $18.80 per day for shelter

... The most expensive places to live in Canada are:

For homeowners,
Toronto	$33.43
Oshawa	$31.47
Ottawa-Hull	$29.60

For renters,
Toronto	$23.43
Vancouver	$22.17
Oshawa	$21.93

on an average day...

From a woman's point of view...

... Top 10 factors women look for when choosing where to live:

low crime rate
clean air
good job prospects
green space
affordable housing
low cost of living
public schools
libraries
universities/colleges
pleasant climate

... Top 15 cities that women choose, based on the above criteria:

Ottawa-Hull
Sherbrooke
Saskatoon
St. John's
London
Winnipeg
Kitchener

on an average day...

Vancouver
Oshawa
Quebec City
Regina
Montreal
Sudbury
Toronto
Thunder Bay

Togetherness...

... 120,000 Canadian families of
three or more generations share
the same residence

on an average day...

A growing concern...

... 10 million square metres of land in Canada are under greenhouse plastic and glass roofing

... 88% of this land is found in British Columbia, Ontario and Quebec

... We buy 1,641,096 garden plants, including 73,973 potted geraniums

NATIONAL HEALTH

on an average day...

Health care in Canada...

... When evaluating Canada's health care system:

44% of Canadians say it has deteriorated
33% of Canadians say it has remained the same
23% of Canadians say it has improved

... The provincial breakdown of those who think our
health care system has deteriorated is as follows:

39% in British Columbia
68% in Alberta
58% in Saskatchewan
42% in Manitoba
40% in Ontario
43% in Quebec
47% in New Brunswick
54% in Nova Scotia
43% in Prince Edward Island
49% in Newfoundland

on an average day...

The cost of health...

... Every man, woman and child spends $4.06 to pay for our national health care plan
... It costs $365 to keep someone in hospital
... Caring for the same patient at home costs $66.67 for the same level of care

... Health care in British Columbia costs $20.4 million, or $850,000 every hour

... Ontario doctors bill OHIP $54,795 for the 2,611 housecalls they make

... 493 ankle x-rays are taken in Ontario, costing OHIP $10,959

on an average day...

... $73,973 is spent by the federal government on direct cancer research

... The Canadian government spends less than $1 per Canadian citizen per year on cancer research; the United States government spends $8 per citizen per year

Hospital zone...

... Sunnybrook Health Science Centre, one of Canada's largest hospitals, has 1,319 beds, 300 doctors, 4,300 other staff and daily operating costs of $713,699

... Ontario hospitals make $90,411 from surgeries and treatments on American patients. This amount is enough to pay the daily wages for 8,000 hospital workers

on an average day...

... Halifax hospitals have "Operation Greenback," an amnesty program to recoup the $822 worth of stolen sheets, towels and surgical greens taken every day. Victoria General Hospital loses $548 worth of linen daily

Under the knife...

... 55 operations are performed at the Hospital for Sick Children in Toronto

... 96 Canadians undergo open-heart surgery

... Pacemakers are surgically implanted in the chests of 27 Canadians
... 75,000 Canadians already have one of these devices inside them

---

on an average day...

... 156 people have their gall bladders removed; 110 of these operations are performed on women. It is the most common surgical procedure in North America, and Canada has the highest rate of gall bladder removal in the Western world

... 29 people have their appendices removed because of acute appendicitis; 8 more people have their appendices removed because of severe yet undiagnosed abdominal pain
... It is estimated that 16 Canadians who really do not need such an operation have their appendices removed

... The risks associated with a general anesthetic are 48 times higher than taking one commuter airline flight. The rate of cardiac arrest with a general anesthetic is 1.7 in 10,000; the mortality rate is 1 in 11,000. There is 1 airline death in 530,000 passenger flights

on an average day...

Operation prime time...

... The Learning Channel's series "The Operation"
attracts 600,000 Canadian viewers, making it one of
the most popular programs on the U.S. specialty networks shown in Canada. Proportionally, it has more
viewers in Canada than in the United States

The ultimate gift...

... Of Canada's 28 million residents, only 7,020,000 have
signed organ donation cards

... 61,779 Canadians are registered with the National
Unrelated Bone Marrow Donor Registry, founded in
1989

on an average day...

... 4 Canadians receive an organ transplant; 3 of these patients receive a kidney

... 2,289 Canadians are on the waiting list for an organ transplant

Of the total,

   2,010 Canadians are waiting for a kidney
   99 need a new heart
   85 need a liver
   60 need a lung
   19 need both a heart and lung(s)
   15 need both a kidney and pancreas
   1 person needs a pancreas

on an average day...

... Those on transplant lists wait:

　　668 days for a kidney(s)
　　315 days for a lung(s)
　　275 days for a heart and lung(s)
　　169 days for a heart
　　115 days for a liver

... The fee schedule set by the Canadian Medical
Association for transplant operations is as follows:

　　$42,405 for a kidney
　　$105,730 for a liver
　　$111,350 for a heart
　　$152,320 for a lung
　　$152,320 for a heart and lung

on an average day...

Are you my type?...

... The Canadian Red Cross collects 1,589 litres of blood from Canadian blood donors in each of the 17 permanent blood centres across the country

... Of the total, 15 litres are donated by patients for the sole purpose of storing blood for themselves for use in an upcoming medical procedure. The blood can be stored for up to five weeks

... On average, out of 100 people eligible to give blood,

46 will have type O
42 will have type A
9 will have type B
3 will have type AB

on an average day...

... 85% of Canadians are Rh positive
... 15% are Rh negative
... 39% are O positive
... 0.45% are AB negative

... 2,603 units of red blood cells are transfused into 822 Canadians

... 300,000 Canadians rely on the blood system to treat their hemophilia

... Canada is the only major industrialized nation that is not self-sufficient in blood fractionation — a process that splits blood plasma into a wide range of products. Canada depends on U.S. suppliers for these products

on an average day...

Take a pill...

... Canada's 64 brand-name drug companies and their 4,000 drug representatives sell $5,205,479 worth of their products

... The companies spend $2,054,795 on lobbying, advertising and promotions to influence the kinds of medical treatment we receive

... Doctors write 547,945 prescriptions for antibiotics. Ampicillin is the most widely prescribed antibiotic in Canada

... Canadians are the world's largest consumers of codeine per capita

on an average day...

... 5 million Canadians take medication worth $1,369,863 for high blood pressure

... 200,000 of these people, according to some experts, do not really have high blood pressure but suffer from "white coat syndrome": these people have normal blood pressure at all times except when they are in the presence of a white-coated medical doctor

... 750,000 women between the ages of 40 and 74 take daily replacement hormone therapy

... 200,000 Canadians take Prozac for symptoms of depression

... Every 4 days, the drug thalidomide is prescribed in Canada for very specific treatments of lupus and bone marrow transplants. The drug is made in Brazil

on an average day...

... 41 requests are made by Canadian doctors to the Emergency Drug Release Program to allow them to prescribe investigational drugs for terminally ill patients

... 500 calls a day are received on toll-free phone lines provided by the Pharmaceutical Manufacturing Association of Canada from consumers seeking information about medications they are taking
... 20% of all requests for information received by the Pharmaceutical Manufacturing Association toll-free phone lines concern hypertension (high blood pressure)

... 4 Canadians die from gastric ulcers and bleeding caused by medications commonly prescribed for arthritis and related disorders

on an average day...

... 32,877 Canadians get some sort of immunization. Of the total, 8 people have adverse reactions that are reported to the Laboratory Centre for Disease Control in Ottawa

In the beginning...

... 18% of all births in Canada are by Caesarean section. Only the United States and Brazil have higher rates of C-sections

on an average day...

... Canadian women buy $21,918 worth of home pregnancy tests

... 250,000 couples in Canada between the ages of 18 and 44 are unable to have children

... 9 women participate in one of Canada's 41 in-vitro fertilization programs offered in 27 hospitals across Canada. Sperm donors are paid $75 each, while recipients pay $125 or more each. One successful pregnancy occurs for every 8 patients who attempt in-vitro fertilization

on an average day...

... 16 children are born who were conceived by sperm from a donor-bank. Only half of the 40 or so artificial insemination programs in Canada will release non-identifying information about donors to the receiving families

Disabling conditions...

... 800,000 Canadians have a mental handicap; 30,000 live in institutions across the country

... 82 Canadians suffer disabling head injuries, many of which result in long-term behavioural and cognitive problems

on an average day...

... 552,585 adult Canadians are visually impaired. Even with eyeglasses they cannot read normal-sized print

... On May 10th, 1994, 10 Montreal-area youths badly damaged their eyes by looking directly at the annular eclipse. One of these youths is now totally blind

... It costs $75.34 for a kidney dialysis patient to be treated at home
... It costs $110.27 for the same treatment in a hospital

... 1.6 million Canadians suffer from bladder incontinence, yet only 1 in 12 has ever sought medical treatment

on an average day...

... 850,000 women have osteoporosis

... 5 new cases of tuberculosis are diagnosed

... 750,000 Canadians wear Medic-Alert bracelets and medallions, which, in the case of an accident, inform medical personnel of pre-existing medical conditions

What's love got to do with it?...

... 5 people are diagnosed with HIV in Metro Toronto

on an average day...

... More than 500 people in Canada do not know that they are infected with the AIDS virus

... There are 444 women living with AIDS, representing 5.8% of AIDS patients in Canada

... 800 women living in Montreal are HIV-positive; 180 of these women have AIDS

... 4 out of 10 Canadian women with HIV or AIDS live in Montreal

... When women are asked how they became HIV-positive:

73% say through heterosexual contact
15% say through IV drug use
12% say through blood transfusions

on an average day...

... When men are asked how they became infected with the AIDS virus:

   83% say through unprotected sex
   9% say through IV drug use
   8% say through blood products

... 7 Canadians die from sexually transmitted Hepatitis B; most of those who die never even know they have the disease
... 250,000 people in Canada are carriers of Hepatitis B

... 137 cases of chlamydia are diagnosed

... An estimated 20% of Canadians have genital herpes

on an average day...

Just a slight adjustment...

... 27,397 people visit their chiropractor. Chiropractic is the third largest primary contact health-care profession after medicine and dentistry

Is it hot in here?...

... 350 Canadian women begin menopause

Seeing food as the enemy...

... According to guidelines set by Health and Welfare Canada, 20% of women and 32% of men are overweight. Yet, when surveyed, 65% of women thought they were overweight, as did 43% of men

on an average day...

... 50% of all women are on a diet; 72% of girls and teens aged 10 to 17 are dieting. Only 5% will be able to keep the weight off, while the other 95% will gain it back, plus extra pounds, within a year

... 50% of all dieters have bulimia or anorexia

... We spend an estimated $139,726 on weight-loss products

Substantial substance abuse...

... Abuse of alcohol and drugs adds $32,876,712 to Canada's health-care costs

on an average day...

... It is estimated that 2,300 doctors practising in Ontario are abusing alcohol and/or drugs

Remodelling ourselves...

... 28 Canadian men undergo cosmetic plastic surgery; the most popular procedure is an eyelid lift

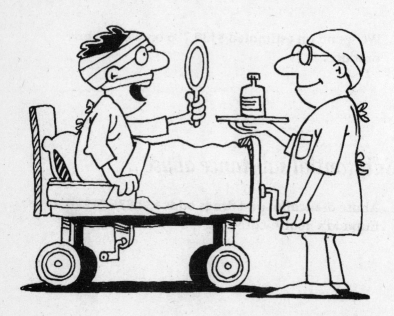

on an average day...

... What it costs to undergo the following cosmetic procedures:

Glycolic acid face peel	$75–$150
Microabrader skin treatment	$200–$300
Laser camouflage	$200–$300
Forehead freeze (Botox injection)	$250
Collagen injections	$400–$800
Chin implant	$1,300
Gore-Tex lip enhancement	$1,500
Cheek implant	$1,900
Nose-tip remodelling	$2,300–$2,700
Eyelid lift (upper and lower)	$2,700

... $5,479 is charged to OHIP for the removal of acne pimples

... Repair of deformed earlobes caused by pierced earrings costs OHIP $5,479 per earlobe

on an average day...

... OHIP pays out $821 to cover doctors' fees for the removal of port wine stains

... OHIP reimburses doctors $191 for cosmetic testicle implants

... $1,425 is charged to OHIP by doctors performing penile implants for impotent patients

Mr. Sandman...

... 5 million Canadians are not getting enough sleep each night, resulting in $16,438,356 in medical costs, industrial accident claims and lost productivity

on an average day...

... 19% of men and 28% of women say it takes them more than 1 hour to fall asleep

... 60% of men and 40% of women over age 60 snore every night

... 13% of all traffic fatalities are caused by drivers falling asleep at the wheel

on an average day...

Bathroom matters...

... 540,000 Canadians suffer from chronic constipation; 360,000 of them are women

... 7% of the adult population are unable to urinate in public washrooms. This is known as the Bashful Bladder Syndrome and can play havoc with social relationships

... More than 60% of Canadians start their day with alcohol; they're not alcoholics, just daily mouthwash users. Most mouthwash contains 22% alcohol by volume

on an average day...

... 3 people are treated at Toronto's Fresh Breath Clinic, one of only two such clinics in North America specializing in the treatment of stubborn mouth odours

... 87,397 toothbrushes are purchased. Toothbrushes should be replaced every 3 months, yet the average Canadian uses only 1.1 toothbrushes per year

Pass the odour eaters...

... Each adult foot produces 250 ml (1 cup) of perspiration

CLAIMS TO FAME

on an average day...

The best country in the world...

... According to the United Nations Human Development Index, based on income, life expectancy and educational attainment, the top 10 countries are:

Canada
Switzerland
Japan
Sweden
Norway
France
Australia
United States
Netherlands
United Kingdom

on an average day...

... The top 15 countries whose citizens have the best daily chances to improve their lives, according to the United Nations Human Development Index, are:

Japan
Canada
Norway
Switzerland
Sweden
United States
Australia
France
Netherlands
United Kingdom
Iceland
Germany
Denmark
Finland
Austria

... Canada's population is growing at a faster rate than that of any other Western industrialized nation. From 1992 to 1993, the population grew by 1.1%

on an average day...

... When *Places Rated Almanac* compared 343 health-care locations in North America, including 21 in Canada, Montreal was rated 13th overall and first in Canada, followed by Halifax, Vancouver and St. John's

Inventive Canadians...

... 32,877 paint rollers are purchased in Canada. Paint rollers are a Canadian invention, introduced in 1940

... 1,370 table hockey games made in Canada are sold in North America. Table hockey is a Canadian invention, introduced in Toronto in 1932

on an average day...

... 5,555 Abdomanizers, a piece of exercise equipment shaped like a blue saucer and invented by a Canadian chiropractor, are purchased

... 16,438 boxes of Trivial Pursuit are sold in 33 countries and in 19 languages. A new edition of cards is produced annually in Canada. Trivial Pursuit is the most successful game ever invented in Canada and accounts for 37% of the adult board-game market in North America

... 3 Blue Armadillos, a shock-absorbing undershirt worn by the likes of Wayne Gretzky, are sold in Canada. They are a Canadian invention

on an average day...

... 1,370 Dipstick Cleaners are sold at a cost of $1.99 each. The Dipstick Cleaner, the invention of two Guelph car dealers, is affixed under the hood of the car; after checking the oil, the user runs the dirty dipstick through the Cleaner's slots and onto its sponge

... Drinkers of Canada Dry Ginger Ale will find half a gram of ginger root in each litre of the soft drink. Canada Dry was patented in Canada in 1906

Made in Canada?...

... 50 Hudson Bay blankets are purchased in Canada. Interestingly, the blankets, which have been around since 1780, have never been made in Canada. They are currently made by John Atkinson and Sons of Pudsey, England

on an average day...

The biggest and the busiest...

... Toronto Hydro is North America's largest municipal utility, with 1,400 employees and 200 linemen

... 1,370 artificial Christmas trees are made by Noma, the world's largest producer

... Gamblers drop $1,428,571 while trying their luck at the Windsor Casino, the world's most profitable casino

... 600 driving students take their test at the John Rhodes Examination Centre in Brampton, the busiest test centre in Canada
... 270 fail

on an average day...

... The stretch of Highway 401 between Highway 427 and Yonge Street in Toronto carries 300,000 cars and is second only to California's Santa Monica Freeway, the most traffic-choked highway in North America

... On each day of the three-day CHIN Picnic in Toronto, the largest annual picnic in the world, 15,000 sausages, 15,000 hot dogs, 8,500 chicken legs and 10,000 pizzas are consumed by 83,400 people

... Toronto's annual Santa Claus Parade, the biggest Christmas parade in the world, attracts 750,000 people along its route, while another 200 million watch on television. U.S. television networks air the parade on American Thanksgiving Day, while Moscow shows the parade twice in December

on an average day...

... The Harbourfront Reading Series in Toronto presents writers from all over the world. More than 1,000 people subscribe to the series, making it the largest literary club in Canada

... During each of the 10 days of the Harbourfront International Festival of Authors in Toronto, 1,200 paying customers attend readings by more than 90 of the world's finest writers. Founded in 1980, the festival is said to be the largest and best of its kind in the world

Well established...

... Redpath Sugar, Canada's oldest sugar company, employs 300 people and refines 1,000 tonnes of raw sugar

on an average day...

... Canada's oldest bookstore, The Book Room in Halifax, which began as a Methodist bookstore in October 1839, no longer has any religious affiliation and now sells all types of books

... 600 books are sold in the Albert Britnell Bookstore in Toronto. It is the oldest bookstore in Canada continuously owned by the same family right up to the present. It is also the only one in Canada that has been located on the same street for 100 years

Uniquely ours...

... Digi Pen Computer Graphic Inc. of Vancouver teaches 100 students from the Vancouver Film School. They offer the only diploma in video game design in North America. Annual tuition is $8,500. They turn away 3 applications for every one they accept

on an average day...

Tiptoe through the tulips...

... 100,000 people attend each day of the annual 6-day Canadian Tulip Festival in Ottawa. More than 6 million bulbs are on display, the largest number in the world outside of Holland

People of note...

... 3 Canadians celebrate their 100th birthday. According to the 1991 Census, Canada has 3,700 citizens aged 100 years or over

on an average day...

... Father Leonard Eugene Boyle, scholar and medievalist from the University of Toronto, can be found in the Vatican as custodian of its vast collection of priceless books and manuscripts. He was appointed by Pope John Paul II in May 1984

... Elli Davis, Royal LePage's top-selling real estate agent for eight consecutive years, sells $100,000 worth of property

... George Cook of Toronto composes 10 to 20 tunes a day. He holds the world record for songwriting: 134,888 to date

on an average day...

Companies of distinction...

... Ortho-McNeil Inc. produces 12,329 IUDs (intrauterine devices) for the United Nations to distribute in 110 countries throughout Asia and Africa

... 548 Tilley hats are made. They come with a lifetime guarantee and are worn by Sir Edmund Hillary, Prince Andrew, Pierre Trudeau and Paul Newman

... Havana House Cigar and Tobacco Merchants Ltd., based in Toronto, sells 2,740 Cuban cigars. Havana House handles the distribution of all Cuban cigars sold in Canada

... When in Toronto, David Letterman buys 6 boxes of Cuban cigars, with 25 cigars per box, from Havana House Cigar and Tobacco Merchants Ltd., at a cost of $1,500

on an average day...

Canadians who care...

... The 1994 M.A.C. Cosmetics Fashion Cares Benefit
donated $125,000 to the AIDS Committee of Toronto.
This donation of the show's proceeds set a record for
the largest single corporate donation from an AIDS
event held in Canada

... The United Way of Greater Toronto, the largest fund-
raising organization in Canada, has 20,000 volunteers
and raises $124,658

... 8,000 participants take part in the annual Manulife
Ride for Heart fundraiser, one of Canada's largest
cycling events, held in Toronto on a Sunday in June.
Pizza Pizza, which donates food for the event, delivers
110 pizzas every 15 minutes

on an average day...

... CIL donates 137 gallons of paint to charities needing to upgrade community buildings and facilities across Canada

... 959 households receive Welcome Wagon gift baskets, delivered by one of 1,200 volunteer hostesses who, since 1930, have been promoting neighbourliness and helpfulness to residents moving into new homes across the country. The gifts are donated by local businesses and services

Incredible edibles...

... The Liquor Control Board of Ontario, the largest retailer of beverage alcohol in the Western world, sells $5,479,452 worth of liquor. The LCBO has 621 stores, 5,000 employees, 2,500 regularly listed wines and spirits and 700 continually changing listings

on an average day...

... Ontario produces 1,095,890 Macintosh apples, which are shipped all over the world. The Mac was discovered in Ontario over 200 years ago; every Mac in the world descends from an Ontario tree

... 70% of the truffle bars made by Tout Sweet Chocolate of Richmond, B.C., are exported to the United States. Tout Sweet's truffle bar won top prize from the Canadian Association of Specialty Foods

on an average day...

... Menu Foods Ltd. of Streetsville, Ontario, the largest private-label canned pet food producer in the world, sells $273,973 worth of their 900 different formulas under 2,200 different labels

Of their total sales,

43% are to the United States
39% remain in Canada
13% are to Japan
5% are to the European and New Zealand markets

... Cantor's Quality Meats and Groceries of Manitoba has been in business for over 50 years. Owner Joe Cantor took on the Milk Marketing Board by selling his milk below the board's floor price. Victorious, today he sells 1,667 litres per day at a bargain price

... Dough Delight Ltd. turns out 1 million bagels, 16,667 kilograms of muffins and 233,333 pita breads. They are the largest Canadian exporter of bread products to the United States

on an average day...

... Woolwich Dairy, near Guelph, Ontario, the largest goat cheese maker in Canada, produces 427 kilograms of goat cheese

... 215,000 ducks reside at King Cole Duck Farm — Canada's largest such farm — in Stouffville, Ontario. There are also 270,000 eggs about to hatch in nine heated incubator buildings

... King Cole Duck Farm processes 5,000 ducks every morning for the market (frozen); they also process 3,000 ducks for the Chinese markets, which insist on fresh birds. The Chinese also want the webbed feet, as they are a dim sum delicacy

... 109,589 Crispy Crunch chocolate bars are sold. They are available in 11 countries and are Canada's favourite chocolate bar

on an average day...

... 1,500 meals are served at the top of Toronto's CN Tower, the world's tallest free-standing restaurant

... During its Thanksgiving food drive, the Daily Bread Food Bank, Canada's largest, collects 77 tonnes of beans, 48 tonnes of macaroni and cheese dinners, 37 tonnes of peanut butter, 17 tonnes of powdered milk and 11 tonnes of baby formula

... The Metro Toronto Zoo, the largest in Canada, spends $1,534 to feed the animals and distributes 2,740 kilograms of food. Menu highlights include Lion's Delight — a 6-kilogram bowl of horsemeat with a side of bones and, occasionally, a defrosted rabbit

on an average day...

Land claims...

... Clayoquot Sound, Canada's largest rain forest, found in a remote part of Vancouver Island, receives 8 mm of rain. Clayoquot Sound covers 260,000 hectares and is home to 100,000 birds and the oldest tree in Canada — a 1,500-year-old red cedar nicknamed The Hanging Garden Tree

... More than 137 people visit the Leslie Street Spit, a peninsula made up of broken asphalt and old telephone poles 20 minutes from downtown Toronto. It is home to 400 species of plants and 280 species of birds, including the world's largest colony of ring-billed gulls, numbering 55,000 pairs

on an average day...

The maple leaf forever...

... Canadiana Textile sells $4,110 worth of Canadian flags to the federal government. A Canadiana Textile flag flies atop the Peace Tower in Ottawa

... Canadian Banners and Flags sells 2,738 Canadian flags

... Canadian Tire is the only national retailer providing a complete line of all sizes of our flag

The Dionnes...

... The Dionne Quintuplets Museum in Callander, Ontario (near North Bay), receives 33 visitors. The museum is located in the log cabin where the world's first surviving set of quintuplets was born

on an average day...

Believe it or not...

... On an average summer night, the "Raccoon Lady of Rosedale," well known to Ministry of Natural Resources officials, allows 30 or more raccoons into the living room of her home. Rosedale is an upper-class neighbourhood of Toronto known for its grand homes

... Jack and Donna Wright of Kingston, Ontario, who own the world's largest number of cats, feed their 689 cats 180 cans of meat and 25 kg of dry cat food ... The cats use 10 litter boxes filled with 20 kg of kitty litter

on an average day...

... On the same day that an ad appeared in the *Toronto Star* for a Toronto doctor who enlarges penises, 157 men booked a surgical consultation. The men, from all across Canada and the United States, will pay $3,000 each for the procedure. Toronto is the only place in North America where this procedure is performed

... At the Queen Street Mental Health Centre, Canada's largest psychiatric hospital, the beauty salon cuts, perms and styles the hair of 20 people. The salon takes appointments from inpatients and outpatients as well as from hospital staff

California dreaming...

... 700,000 Canadians live in Los Angeles, California

on an average day...

Notable neighbourhoods...

... The postal codes with the highest percentages of people with incomes of $100,000 or more are:

	Number of Residents Earning $100,000 or More	Percentage of Total Residents
H3Y Westmount, Quebec	1,250	18
L4G 3G8 Aurora, Ontario	140	17
M4W Toronto (Rosedale)	1,250	17
T3E 6W3 Calgary	160	15
M4N Toronto (Bridle Path)	1,450	15
M2P Toronto (York Mills)	600	14
M4T Toronto (Moore Park)	930	14
M2L Toronto (Bayview North)	1,000	13
M4V Toronto (Russell Hill)	1,420	13
M5P Toronto (Forest Hill)	1,740	13

PROVINCIAL AFFAIRS

on an average day...

Parlez-vous français?...

... When Canadians are asked what their mother tongue
is, 6,502,865 say French. Of these,

48,835 live in British Columbia
53,715 live in Alberta
20,885 live in Saskatchewan
49,130 live in Manitoba
485,395 live in Ontario
5,556,105 live in Quebec
241,565 live in New Brunswick
36,635 live in Nova Scotia
5,590 live in Prince Edward Island
2,770 live in Newfoundland
865 live in the Yukon
1,375 live in the Northwest Territories

Pacifically speaking...

... 1 tremor (which most residents never feel) occurs
somewhere along the Pacific coast of British
Columbia, Canada's most active earthquake area.
Most are simply felt by seismotic instruments

on an average day...

... Marijuana is British Columbia's most profitable crop, taking in $2,054,795 in illegal sales

... 498,630 kilograms of cranberries are grown in Richmond, B.C., representing 80% of all cranberries grown in Canada

... The annual World Championship Bathtub Race takes place in Nanaimo on the fourth Sunday in July. The race is 34 miles long and was first run in 1967. For information, write to: Loyal Nanaimo Bathtub Society, P.O. Box 565, Nanaimo, B.C. V9R 5L5

on an average day...

... With 3 bathtubs per capita, Nanaimo, B.C., is known
as the bathtub capital of the world

... 46% of all B.C. homes have a fireplace — the highest
percentage in Canada
... Prince Edward Island has the lowest number with 11%

... The British Columbia Automobile Association (BCAA),
founded in 1906, is Canada's largest and oldest automobile club. It now has 450,000 members in 16 service
chapters throughout the province

... The ferry from Kootenay Bay to Balfour in B.C. is the
longest free ferry ride in the world

on an average day...

... There are 40 manned lighthouses along the British Columbia coast, as well as 440 beacons, 480 buoys and 110 foghorns

... Kootenay National Park is the only national park in Canada where visitors can see both glaciers and cacti

... Fairmont Hot Springs, in East Kootenay District, attracts 2,055 visitors and uses 1 million gallons of odourless mineral water. Fairmont is the largest and most popular year-round resort on the western side of the Rockies

... The odds of winning the Lotto B.C. jackpot are 1 in 3,838,380

on an average day...

... Parking meters in Vancouver are fed $16,438 worth of coins, which go into the city's coffers

... In British Columbia there are 53 phone lines per 100 people, the most of any province in Canada. The national average is 48.9 lines

... Cruise ships stopping at the Port of Vancouver on their way to Alaska carry 1,611 passengers

Prairie ponderings...

... Albertans own the most televisions per household, as well as the most telephones, VCRs, camcorders, cars, downhill skis and overnight camping equipment

on an average day...

... The Alberta government spends $685 on rat control
... Alberta is the only major populated place in the world
that is essentially free of rats. A rat is seen only once
every 33 days in the province

... The 17,000 oil-producing wells in Alberta provide 90%
of the total Canadian crude oil, natural gas and natural gas by-products

on an average day...

... Visitors to the West Edmonton Mall, the world's largest shopping complex, can spend their money in 800 different places, including:

210 fashion shops for women
35 menswear stores
55 shoe stores
35 jewellery shops
19 movie theatres
110 restaurants
a par-46, 18-hole mini-golf course

... 30,000 cars can park in one of two lots outside the West Edmonton Mall

... 4,500 tourists in Jasper, Alberta, take a ride on buses that have shoulder-high tires to enable them to take in the grandeur of the Columbia Icefield

... Edmonton has a 98% chance of having a white Christmas

on an average day...

... Saskatchewan residents own the most microwave
ovens, gas barbecues and freezers per capita in
Canada

... The Saskatchewan Wheat Pool spends $1,918 on pest
control

... Harden & Huyse of Saskatoon use 120 kilograms of
Belgian chocolate to make their famous chocolates,
available from Victoria to Quebec

... Altona, Manitoba, is the Sunflower Capital of Canada
and provides Canadians with most of their sunflower
seeds

on an average day...

... There are twice as many beavers living in Manitoba as there are people

Ontario — yours to discover...

... 55 Ontarians legally change their name, the highest number of name-droppers in the country. It costs $137 to change your name (maximum 66 characters, including spaces, apostrophes and hyphens)

... 4 animals are put down because of rabies in Ontario, where more animals are diagnosed with the disease than anywhere else in North America

... With more than 35,000 participants, Toronto has the greatest number of windsurfers per capita in North America

on an average day...

... Ontario Hydro uses 50% more electricity in its own buildings than the entire city of Toronto uses, and it doesn't have to pay for it

... 725,000 litres of tomato paste are produced at the Heinz plant in Leamington, Ontario. Every tomato used in a Heinz product in Canada goes through the Leamington plant

... 1,429 personalized vanity licence plates are issued at a cost of $106 each in Ontario

... Ontario drivers can now sport the logo of an Ontario sports team on their licence plates, or they can choose the provincial emblem, flower or bird
... Brand new non-personalized plates bearing a full-colour logo cost $51.10

on an average day...

... Brand new personalized plates with a full-colour logo cost $185.85

... 150 orders are placed to have existing plates reissued with a full-colour logo at a cost of $185.85

Logos include, in order of popularity:

The Toronto Maple Leafs
the provincial bird — a loon
The Toronto Blue Jays
the provincial flower — a trillium
The Toronto Raptors
The Hamilton Tiger Cats
The Ottawa Senators
The Toronto Argonauts
The Ottawa Roughriders

La belle province...

... 100,000 people attend each day of the annual ten-day Quebec Winter Carnival, the largest winter carnival in the world and the oldest in Canada

... $5 million in revenue is collected during each day of the carnival

on an average day...

... Quebeckers own more life insurance than anyone else in North America

... Despite their strong Roman Catholic Church heritage, Quebec has the highest rate of single-parent families, common-law unions and divorce

... Quebec has the lowest birthrate in Canada

... Quebeckers eat the most imported cheese and red wine per capita in Canada

on an average day...

... Quebeckers are Canada's largest consumers of gin;
   English Canada prefers rye

... Quebec is the only market in North America where
   Pepsi is Number 1 in the non-diet-cola segment

... Barbecue and dill-flavoured potato chips are preferred
   in Quebec; the salt and vinegar variety is tops outside
   the province

... Quebeckers own fewer credit cards and owe less
   money on the ones they do own

on an average day...

... Quebeckers buy the most lottery tickets per capita in Canada

... Quebeckers take fewer prescription drugs per capita than other Canadians, but use more soft tranquillizers, such as Valium

... Quebeckers own the most cross-country skis in the country

on an average day...

... Quebeckers make the fewest long distance calls

... 70% of Quebeckers bank at co-operatively owned credit unions (les caisses populaires Desjardins)

... 90% of Quebec's most popular television shows are produced in the province

... The top-rated television program in Quebec in October 1993 was the Quebec-made drama *Blanche*, while a World Series baseball game was favoured outside the province

on an average day...

Maritime musings...

... Every resident in New Brunswick has free voice-mail on his or her home telephone, provided by the phone company. The caller is charged 25 cents to leave a message

... 82 New Brunswickers apply for moose-hunting licences over the telephone — a new touch-tone service

... Through their telephones, New Brunswick residents are provided with a high-tech warning system that automatically calls numbers in areas threatened by natural disasters or crime

... 55 cruise ship passengers arrive at the port of Saint John

on an average day...

... Since 1868, the Eclectic Reading Club of Saint John has met on the last Thursday of every month to discuss books. It is the oldest, and most formal, reading club in Canada; protocol requires men to wear black tie and women to wear good dresses

... 36,986 kilograms of wild blueberries, worth $109,589, are harvested by growers belonging to the Nova Scotia Blueberry Growers Association

on an average day...

... Bruce Rand of Annapolis Valley, Nova Scotia, grows $2,739 worth of broccoli. He has one of the country's largest crops of broccoli

... More than 15,000 Japanese tourists make an annual pilgrimage to Anne of Green Gables' famous home in Prince Edward Island. After World War II, *Anne of Green Gables* became compulsory reading in Japanese schools

... In Poland, a musical based on L.M. Montgomery's novel, *The Blue Castle*, plays to full houses every night and was voted the country's most popular musical in 1994

... The annual four-day Alberton Spudster Winter Carnival in Prince Edward Island is overseen by Spudster, the half-potato, half-lobster carnival mascot. Highlights of the carnival include a fancy-dress skate and a sliding party

on an average day...

... Newfoundlanders report having sex an average of 10 times per month, the highest amount in the country. The national average is 7 times per month

... On November 5 of each year (Guy Fawkes Day), Newfoundlanders burn 146,000 tires in 10,000 bonfires to commemorate the ill-fated attempt to blow up the British Parliament in 1605

THAT'S ENTERTAINMENT

on an average day...

Reel time...

... The film industry in Canada generates $2,739,726.
Toronto is the third largest centre for filmmaking in
North America, following Los Angeles and New York.
It costs $35,000 to film an episode of a television show
in Toronto compared with $75,000 in New York
... 7 filming location permits are issued for the Toronto
area

... Film and television production in Ontario generates
$926,027 in business, most of which is spent in Toronto

... Film and television production in British Columbia
generates $783,562 for the province. Most of the
money is spent in Vancouver

on an average day...

Video views...

... Only 33% of people who enter a video store know what video they want to rent before they go in

... 24 pirated video cassettes are seized by police in raids across the country

on an average day...

On the tube...

... Only 2,758,000 households out of 10,000,000 do not have cable television

... TV Ontario produces 2 hours and 20 minutes of original programming

... TVO, which is publicly funded, receives $10,959 from its 72,000 Canadian members

... WNED Channel 17 in Buffalo, N.Y., collects $17,014 from its 75,500 Canadian members

... The CBC and CTV networks provide 3 hours of close-captioned television programs, while American networks provide 41 hours of close-captioned programming

on an average day...

... Canadian broadcasters lose $342,466 in infomercial revenue to American television stations

... CTV's talk show, *Shirley*, hosted by Shirley Solomon, is seen by 350,000 viewers

... Shirley Solomon receives 27 fan letters, more than anyone else at the network

... On May 20, 1993, 33,323 fans of *Cheers* crowded into Toronto's SkyDome to watch the final episode on the Jumbotron screen. While there was no charge to get in, 23,000 kilograms of food were collected for the Daily Bread Food Bank

on an average day...

Have you heard?...

... Canadians spend $2 million on recorded music

... We buy 47,857 pre-recorded cassette tapes

... 5,479 Garth Brooks CDs and cassettes are sold

... 548 copies of Michelle Wright's album *Now and Then* are sold

... 274 copies of *Everybody Knows* by Prairie Oyster are purchased

... 137 copies of Ian Tyson's album *And Stood There Amazed* are sold

... Canadians buy 68 copies of Bing Crosby's *Merry Christmas* album, first released in 1942

... 129 copies of the rereleased CD version are sold

on an average day...

... Georges Hamel, a 46-year-old guitar player from Drummondville, Quebec, sells 98 copies of his 19 French-language country albums

... 1,438 portable/personal CD players are purchased

... 187,000 Canadians listen to CBC Radio's *As It Happens*; this represents 10% of all Canadians listening to the radio between 6:30 p.m. and 8:00 p.m. EST

... There are 95 country music stations operating in Canada. CISS-FM ranks third overall in the very competitive Toronto radio market, with 770,008 listeners. More impressively, CISS-FM is the third largest country music station in North America. New York's WYNY is first and Chicago's WUSN is second

on an average day...

... When business people are asked what radio station they listen to in the morning (between 6:00 a.m and 10:00 a.m.):

Vancouverites favour CKNW with 25.3% of the potential market; CBU is second with 22%
In Toronto, 18.6% of the market tune into CHFI; 17.5% listen to CHUM-FM
In Montreal, the top French-language choice is CBF, with 21.2% of the French market, while the top English-language choice is CJAD, with 30.5% of the English market

Read this...

... Canadians buy 501,370 magazines

... 81,429 copies of *Maclean's* magazine are purchased. Each copy sold is read by 5 people

on an average day...

... 25,714 copies of *Sports Illustrated* are sold

... 3,000 Canadians subscribe to *The Old Fart*, a magazine for and about curmudgeons

... Canadians buy $273,973 worth of comic books. Sim's *Cerebus*, published in Kitchener, Ontario, is Canada's most successful entry with a 0.2% share of the North American market

on an average day...

... The Knitting Guild of Canada publishes *Knitter's Forum*, a quarterly newsletter for avid knitters. An annual subscription costs $32.10

... There are 3 daily Chinese-language newspapers published in Canada with circulations of over 29,000 each. They are *World Journal Daily News*, *Sing Tao Jih Pao* and *Ming Pao Daily News*

... 1,333 Europeans read *Canada Journal*, a bimonthly magazine catering to the fascination that Germans, Austrians and Swiss feel for Canada. It is a German-language magazine, printed in Germany

... Toronto public libraries collect $1,532 in fines on 2,386 overdue books

on an average day...

... Only 15,000 of the 90,000 new Canadian books published each year are available in the average mall chain bookstore

... The average well-stocked independent bookstore carries about 30,000 of these new titles

... In its first 7 months in Canadian bookstores, James Redfield's *The Celestine Prophecy* sold 334 copies daily. It is a slim, easy-to-read mystical thriller about an ancient Peruvian manuscript that promises nine insights for self-fulfillment and transcendent union with the universe

... 667 copies of David Chilton's *The Wealthy Barber* are sold. It has been on the national bestseller lists for the last six years

on an average day...

... 82 copies of W.O. Mitchell's classic 1947 novel, *Who Has Seen The Wind*, are sold

Live on stage...

... 6,849 people watch a performance of Canada's Cirque du Soleil

on an average day...

... 37,260 Canadians take in one of 106 live performances by theatre, dance and other arts companies across the country

... Each performance of Toronto's mega-musical *Phantom of the Opera* costs $85,714 to stage

... During each day of its run, $225,000 worth of tickets to the production of *Show Boat* at the Ford Centre for the Performing Arts Centre in North York were sold

Do not pass Go, do not collect $200...

... 822 Monopoly games are sold in Canada

on an average day...

Impressive numbers...

... On each of its 120 days, 4,976 people viewed the
Barnes Exhibit at the Art Gallery of Ontario, bringing
in $20,000 worth of ticket sales. The exhibit featured
83 paintings by Renoir, Cezanne, Matisse and other
Post-Impressionist artists

LET'S EAT!

on an average day...

The staff of life...

... We eat 2,465,753 loaves of bread, or about 60 million slices

... 45 million of these slices hold some sort of sandwich filling

Tea time...

... We drink 19,178,082 cups of tea

Something fishy...

... British Columbia Packers Ltd., purveyors of Cloverleaf canned salmon, went fishing for statistics and found a whopper: 40% of Canadians object to unwanted skin and bones in their salmon. Yet only 10% of all canned salmon is boneless and skinless due to the higher costs of production

on an average day...

Fowl play...

... 21,918 turkeys are born at Ontario turkey farms, which produce 40% of the Canadian total

Pass the pasta...

... Canadians eat 273,973 kilograms of pasta, worth about $191,780

Cukiness...

... Canadians eat 504,000 cucumbers — 350 cukes a minute!

on an average day...

A lot of fungi...

... Money's Mushrooms, the country's largest producer of fresh and processed mushrooms, sells $13,699 worth of the fungi

Honey, honey...

... 86,991 kilograms of honey are produced, making Canada the sixth largest producer of honey in the world. Although honey is produced in all of the provinces and territories, Alberta leads the country, followed by Saskatchewan and Manitoba

... Due to our climate, an average of 59 kilograms of honey are produced from each beehive in Canada, twice the world average

on an average day...

For our health...

... We purchase $479,452 worth of health foods. Of the total, $16,438 is spent on rice cakes

Gourmet goodies...

... Canadians consume 2,500 kilograms of imported escargot

... We import $95,890 worth of olive oil; 90% of it is extra virgin quality

on an average day...

Something kosher...

... 75% of all kosher food sold in Canada is purchased by non-Jewish people

Something sweet...

... 440,959 kilograms of cookies are produced

Of the total,

221,685 kilograms are chocolate mallow cookies
72,887 are plain biscuits
62,561 are assorted
53,755 are sandwich type with fillings
30,071 are chocolate coated

... 64,286 boxes of the Girl Guides of Ontario new chocolate mint cookies, worth $164,286, were sold each day of a two week campaign over Christmas

on an average day...

... If we could buy Girl Guide sandwich cookies every day of the year, we would buy 16,438 boxes

... Canadians lick up $958,904 worth of ice cream

... Häagen-Dazs produces 9,863 500-ml tubs of ice cream; Honey Vanilla is the most popular flavour in Canada

... Gelato Fresco produces 5,000 500-ml tubs of its ice cream-like product in 13 flavours

... Dalton's, the largest processor of coconut in Canada, processes 6,227 kilograms of coconut

on an average day...

... The Sun Rype plant in Kelowna processes 124,273 kilograms of B.C. fruit
... The company also makes enough pie filling to bake 4,110 pies and produces 40,000 cases of fruit juice

... 364 tonnes of specialty chocolates are produced in Canada

... 45% of all bubble gum sold in Canada is Bubblicious, which outsells its nearest rival 2 to 1

on an average day...

... Concord Confections makes 10,958,904 Tongue Splashers, a type of gum with flavours such as Slime Green and Bleeding Red. While the candy is made in Ontario, it cannot be sold in Canada because it contains too much food colouring

You can't eat only one...

... Canadians buy $41,369,863 worth of potato chips

Oh, I forgot my list...

... An average grocery shopping excursion takes 45 minutes, involves 32 items and costs about $86

on an average day...

... When Canadians visit a grocery store, the top 10 most popular items they purchase are:

soft drinks
ready-to-eat cereals
cookies
toilet paper
fruit juices
laundry detergent
frozen beverages
ice cream
eggs
canned soup

... There is 1 grocery store for every 865 Canadians, compared to 1 store for every 1,816 Americans

... 32% of Canadian grocery stores offer bulk foods, compared to 24% of U.S. food stores
... 32% of Canadian grocery stores sell greeting cards, compared to 88% of American stores

on an average day...

... 12% of Canadian grocery stores have photofinishing services, compared to 82% in the United States
... 6% of Canadian grocery stores rent videos, compared to 57% of American stores

In the kitchen cupboards of the nation...

... The 10 most popular items in the average Canadian pantry are:

baking powder
baking soda
white sugar
vanilla extract
salt
all-purpose flour
cinnamon
brown sugar
fresh apples
cornstarch

on an average day...

... The 10 most popular pantry items in the United States are:

> white sugar
> black pepper
> salt
> ketchup
> baking soda
> cinnamon
> all-purpose flour
> vanilla
> peanut butter
> potatoes

... More than 67% of Canadians have a bag of semi-sweet chocolate chips tucked away in a cupboard behind their granola. Only 35% of our American neighbours keep chocolate chips in their pantry

... 64% of all Canadians have a bottle of Heinz ketchup in their kitchen cupboard

on an average day...

... Canadians buy 879,726 cans of soup, 166,027 packages of dry soup and 120,822 cups of instant noodles. It is estimated that every Canadian household has 9 tins of soup in the kitchen cupboard on any given day

Sugar and spice...

... 27,397 tonnes of sugar are produced from sugar beet crops grown in Canada

... We consume the equivalent of 246,575 75-g bottles of herbs and spices

on an average day...

Of these, the 10 most popular are:

black pepper
garlic salt/powder
onion flakes/powder
parsley leaves
oregano
basil
cinnamon
ginger
chili powder
cumin

Recipes for success...

... 90 copies of *The Canadian Living Cookbook* are sold

... 3,571 copies of *The David Nichol Cookbook* were sold each day in its first month of publication. It is the fastest-selling Canadian cookbook of all time

on an average day...

Wine, beer and spirits...

... Hillebrand Wines of Ontario produces 740 cases of its 30 different wines

... According to David Goldberg, professor of clinical bio-chemistry at the University of Toronto, Ontario red wines contain almost twice as much resveratrol as red wines from California, Australia and Italy and three times as much resveratrol as red wines from South America. Resveratrol helps reduce blood clotting and may boost production of so-called "good cholesterol," which does not block blood flow

... 410,959 Bloody Caesars are consumed in Canada
... 70% of all Clamato juice sold in Canada is bought for this purpose. The cocktail was invented in 1969 by a bartender working in Marco's Italian Restaurant in Calgary, Alberta

on an average day...

... 164,384 bottles of Labatt Ice Beer are consumed in Japan

... 35 million cardboard beer cases are in circulation in Canada at any given time

Menu choices...

... The most popular menu items in Canadian restaurants are soft drinks, ordered 21% of the time, and French fries, ordered 19% of the time

RECREATIONAL
PURSUITS

on an average day...

Batter up...

... 50,617 fans jam SkyDome to watch the Toronto Blue Jays

... Attending a Toronto Blue Jays home game at SkyDome can cost a family of four approximately $140, the most expensive baseball outing in the major leagues:

Average ticket	$14.25 x 4
1 14-oz beer	$ 4.50 x 2
1 soft drink	$ 1.74 x 4
1 regular hotdog	$ 1.99 x 4
Skydome parking	$15.00 x 1
Souvenir baseball cap	$14.00 x 2
Official program	$ 5.00 x 2

on an average day...

... The average major league baseball player earns $2,867

... The following is a baseball player's average daily take on the 10 major league teams with the highest average salaries:

Toronto Blue Jays	$5,896
Cincinnati Reds	$5,469
New York Yankees	$5,448
Kansas City Royals	$5,189
Atlanta Braves	$5,018
Los Angeles Dodgers	$4,999
New York Mets	$4,940
Oakland Athletics	$4,938
Chicago Cubs	$4,735
Detroit Tigers	$4,596

... Toronto's SkyDome is the country's busiest sports stadium, with 16,712 visitors

on an average day...

... SkyDome's Jumbotron generates $16,438 in advertising revenue. SkyDome charges advertisers $822 a day for a complete package of spots during Jays games and all other events

... Toronto's SkyDome sells 100 bottles of number 15 sunscreen

... 4,686,000 Canadians watched on television each of the final 4 games of the 1993 World Series

... Roberto Alomar of the Toronto Blue Jays ruins 2 bats per game, the most of any player in the major leagues

on an average day...

The puck stops here...

... Of the 609 players on the 24 NHL teams during the 1992–93 season, 403 (66%) were Canadian, a drop from 71% in the previous season

... The Toronto Maple Leafs hockey franchise is worth $63 million (U.S.). The Leafs are the seventh most valuable team in the NHL, behind Detroit, Boston, New York (Rangers), Montreal, Los Angeles and Chicago

... The attendance at a home game of each of Canada's 7 NHL teams is:

19,719 for the Calgary Flames
17,005 for the Montreal Canadiens
16,179 for the Edmonton Oilers
15,769 for the Vancouver Canucks
15,586 for the Toronto Maple Leafs
13,666 for the Quebec Nordiques
12,931 for the Winnipeg Jets

on an average day...

ROWS 18 - 48

... 3,334 empty cigarette packages are found after a hockey game in the Montreal Forum. Smoking is officially banned anywhere inside the Forum

... 1,370 people visit the Hockey Hall of Fame in Toronto

... 16,438 hockey sticks are purchased

on an average day...

... The world's biggest hockey stick manufacturer, Karhu Canada, sells 1,370 sticks in Quebec alone under the names Titan, Koho and Canadien

... 548 hockey pucks are made by Baron Rubber of St-Jérôme, Quebec, the exclusive supplier of all NHL pucks

... 16 pairs of skates are donated to Project Arctic Ice Skate, a group dedicated to gathering new and used skates and hockey equipment for distribution to 41 communities in Canada's North

Skating figures...

... 232 Canadians participate in speed skating

on an average day...

... 1 person joins the other 190,000 Canadians who are members of the Canadian Figure Skating Association. 75% of the membership is made up of children in learn-to-skate programs

... On March 9, 1995, almost 2 million Canadians watched Elvis Stojko win his second consecutive World Men's Figure Skating Championship, broadcast from Birmingham, England

A bevy of bonspiels...

... 66,667 Canadians curl in one of 700 curling clubs across Canada

... 6 million curling fans watch, on television, Canada's best male curlers compete in the Brier

on an average day...

It's all downhill from here...

... 1,644 lift tickets are sold at B.C.'s Whistler Mountain. Of the total, 132 are for snowboarders

... $1,121 worth of snowboards and accessories are sold by Luxury Snowboards Inc. in Vancouver, B.C.

A misnomer...

... 540,000 Canadians suffer from tennis elbow. Of the sufferers, only 27,000 actually play tennis

on an average day...

A touchy subject...

... 38,105 Canadians play touch football, according to Football Canada, the national governing body of amateur football. Of the total, 4,355 are women

Playing around...

... 142,466 rounds of golf are played in Canada

... 702,000 Canadians own a set of golf clubs

... On average, it costs $25 to play 18 holes of golf at public and semi-private courses in Canada; 3.9 million Canadians play regularly

on an average day...

... The average cost of a round of 18 holes of golf at a public course around the world:

$150 in Japan
$96 in Spain
$64 in the Bahamas
$57 in France and Germany
$42 in Britain and Italy
$35 in Canada
$30 in the United States
$16 in Mexico
$7 in Iran

... The Dynamic Golf Centre in Thornhill, Ontario, regrips 178 golf clubs at an average price of $7 per club

The horsey set...

... 822 people from all over the world visit the 300-acre Spruce Meadows Equestrian Centre near Calgary, Alberta

on an average day...

... 140,000 Canadians travel to Churchill Downs in Louisville, Kentucky, to watch the annual run for the roses

Pedal power...

... 814,286 adult cyclists ride bikes. The most dangerous place to ride a bicycle is in downtown Toronto, where more than 400,000 motorists compete with 40,000 cyclists, resulting in a cycling fatality every 5 days

... Ottawa has North America's highest number of daily cyclists per capita — 270,000 riders

on an average day...

... 700 Ontarians are licensed by the Ontario Cycling Association to participate in more than 40 annual mountain bike races. The British Columbia Cycling Association has more than 900 members who also compete in these races

... $2,055 worth of halogen bicycle lights are sold by BLT Light Systems in Nelson, B.C.

Riding the waves...

... 1 handmade sailboard is sold by Roberts High Performance Sailboards in North Vancouver, B.C. Each sailboard costs $1,800 (U.S.) and takes 28 hours to make

... 15,000 Canadians participate in rowing for exercise
... There are 72 rowing clubs across the country

on an average day...

... 20,000 Canadians spend a summer day bouncing off the water on a Jet Ski or similar personal watercraft

Take a hike...

... 52 people hike the West Coast Trail in Pacific Rim National Park on Vancouver Island. The trail is so popular that Parks Canada had to impose a limit on the number of people using it each day. Hikers make reservations for the summer season, at a $25 booking fee, on a 1-800 line

... 80% of the spaces are booked during the first week that the phone line is open

on an average day...

... 1,370 people hike the Bruce Trail in the Niagara Escarpment. In 1990, the United Nations declared the trail, which stretches from the Niagara River to Lake Huron along an ancient sea, to be a World Biosphere Reserve, a distinction it shares with the Galapagos Islands, Africa's Serengeti Plain and the Florida Everglades

Genteel sports...

... 179 people in Ontario participate in lawn bowling

... 30,000 students belong to the 25-year-old Taoist Tai Chi Society. One study found that 80% of elderly people who practise Tai Chi can touch their toes, compared to only 20% to 30% of elderly people who do not

on an average day...

Strictly for the birds...

... 1.2 million Canadians consider themselves serious birders, able to identify more than 100 species

... An additional 3.6 million Canadians describe themselves as casual backyard bird-watchers

... There are 580 species of birds native to Canada

... Point Pelee, on Lake Erie at the southernmost tip of Canada's mainland, receives 1,438 bird-watching enthusiasts from around the world. On an average day in May, birders spend $67,742 in the national park and in three adjacent communities

... The average Canadian birder earns $156 in his or her regular day job; 60% of birders have a university degree and 10% of those hold a Ph.D.

on an average day...

... It costs $859 to outfit oneself with the equipment required for bird-watching:

$350 for a telescope
$220 for a tripod
$100 for binoculars
$85 for a bug hat and vest
$79 for a rain guard
$25 for a field guide

On a wing and a prayer...

... 2,000 mostly middle-aged or older men enjoy pigeon racing

... 3,000 birds participate in the Upper Canada National 400 Miler, Ontario pigeon racing's equivalent of the Kentucky Derby

on an average day...

Not playing fair...

... 6 Canadian athletes undergo drug testing; 1 athlete tests positive for a banned substance

... 984 youngsters between the ages of 11 and 18 use either painkillers or stimulants to enhance their athletic performance

... 30,000 Canadian males aged 16 to 18 use anabolic steroids

When asked why they use them,

53% say to improve athletic ability
47% say to change their physique

on an average day...

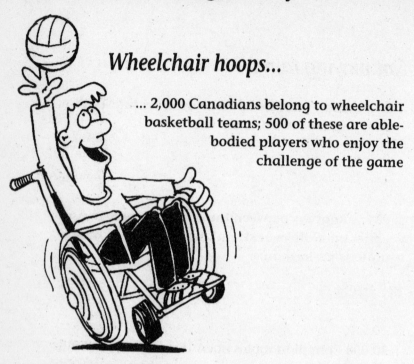

Wheelchair hoops...

... 2,000 Canadians belong to wheelchair basketball teams; 500 of these are able-bodied players who enjoy the challenge of the game

Wheelchair seating...

... The number of wheelchair spaces available for Canadians with disabilities attending the following sport venues are:

300 at Toronto's SkyDome for Blue Jays baseball games
98 at Olympic Saddledome for a Calgary Flames hockey game
49 at Northlands Coliseum, home of the Edmonton Oilers

on an average day...

48 at Pacific Coliseum for Vancouver Canucks hockey games

30 at Winnipeg Arena for a Winnipeg Jets game

22 at Ottawa Civic Centre for Senators hockey games

20 at Colisée for Quebec Nordiques hockey games

6 at Montreal Forum for a Canadiens hockey game

4 at Maple Leaf Gardens for Toronto Maple Leaf games

Fit facts...

... 80% to 90% of Canadians say they believe in the importance of fitness, but only 11% stick to a routine that provides the recommended minimum amount of exercise — 30 minutes of intensive aerobic exercise, 3 to 4 times per week

on an average day...

Olympic appetites...

... 100 cases of coffee and 20 cases of peanut butter were shipped to Lillehammer for the Canadian Olympic Team's 16 days in Norway

Among my souvenirs...

... A Blue Jays Championship leather jacket costs $2,400
... A lithograph of Edmonton Eskimos quarterback Damon Allen costs $1,204
... A replica of the Queen's baton from the Commonwealth games costs $295
... A Canada Cup Challenge 1994 necktie retails for $100
... A Toronto Raptors cap is priced at $30
... A Calgary Stampede belt buckle is priced at $15

ON THE GO

on an average day...

Come fly with me...

... Canada has 58,944 licensed pilots, 27,912 registered aircraft and 748 public airports

... 5,479 air passengers fly between Toronto, Ottawa and Montreal

... 1,918 tonnes of cargo are sent by air

... Air Canada has 450 flights, yet loses $1 million

... Toronto's Island Airport, located in downtown Toronto, handles 50 commercial flights and 446 passengers

on an average day...

... Canadian Airlines spends $216,438 on its in-flight meals

... Canadian Airlines spends $10.94 per passenger on food and drink, although those costs are not evenly apportioned among economy class and business class passengers

... The Cara flight kitchen at Halifax airport produces 3,500 meals

... Twice a day, a bird flies into the engine of a commercial jet in Canada, causing potentially disastrous results

on an average day...

Incentive travel...

... 1,334 people join a frequent flyer program offered by one of Canada's airlines

... 3 million Canadians are already members of such a club

... It takes 10,000 Aeroplan Miles to receive a 2 for 1 deal on a short-haul business class ticket in Canada. A resident of Dhaka, Bangladesh, must kill 10,000 rats to get a free colour television from the Bangladesh government. (To collect the television, rat catchers need only turn in the rat's tail)

... 5,479 tails are redeemed daily

On the road to...

... According to the Canadian Automobile Association, the top 10 driving vacation destinations are:

Orlando, Florida
Los Angeles, California

on an average day...

Phoenix, Arizona
Myrtle Beach, Florida
Vancouver, British Columbia
Miami, Florida
Toronto, Ontario
Old Orchard, Maine
The Maritimes
Banff/Jasper, Alberta

Commuting...

... Vancouverites spend 1 hour getting to and from their jobs, the most time spent in the country
... Torontonians average 59 minutes getting to and from work
... Montrealers average 54 minutes in their commute
... People living in Ottawa-Hull spend 51 minutes in transit
... Winnipeggers take 51 minutes to get to and from work
... Haligonians spend the least time getting to and from their jobs: only 38 minutes

on an average day...

... 60% of Canadians use their car to get to work
... 20% of Canadians walk to work
... 10% use public transit
... 2% cycle
... 8% use more than one form of transit

Wheel luxury...

... At the 3 Rolls-Royce dealerships in Canada, prices start at $212,300 for the Silver Spirit III and rise to $433,400 for the Silver Spur III Touring Limousine ... It costs $3,200 to replace the "Flying Lady" hood ornament on a Rolls-Royce. The ornament is officially known as the Spirit of Ecstasy

on an average day...

... Canadians buy 2 Jaguars; Americans buy 35; world-wide, 75 are sold

Wheel sporty...

... 447 Canadians buy a minivan

... 2 Canadians purchase a Harley-Davidson motorbike

Changing hands...

... 9,589 used cars change ownership. Of the total, 7,671 are sold privately

on an average day...

... 27 Canadians buy a new car that turns out to be a "lemon"

Free wheeling...

... 274 used cars are driven across the U.S. border into Canada duty-free

Now you see it...

... Car thefts per day:

398 in Canada
71 in the greater Toronto area
47 in Montreal
18 in Calgary
14 in Edmonton
14 in Hamilton-Wentworth
14 in Winnipeg
13 in Vancouver
9 in Ottawa

on an average day...

... 43% of stolen cars are left running, have the keys in the ignition or are unlocked

... The most frequently stolen cars are:

Ford Mustang Cobra GT
Volkswagen Golf 2-door
Suzuki Sidekick Soft Top
Volkswagen Golf 4-door
Suzuki Sidekick 4-door Hard Top
Honda Civic 2-door
Jeep YJ
Ford Mustang LX
Chevy/GMC Tracker Soft Top 4WD
Chevy/GMC Tracker Soft Top 2WD

on an average day...

Driving costs...

... The cost of renewing a driver's licence and registration, based on a 1993 Ford Taurus GL, 4-door, 6-cylinder sedan, is highest in Montreal at $182 and least expensive in Regina at $48. The average Canadian pays $81

Under the hood...

... 109,589 people change the oil in their cars

... When Canadians are asked, "If someone doing repair work on your vehicle offered to lower their fee by 20% if you pay cash to avoid taxes," the percentage in each province who would accept the offer are as follows:

57% in British Columbia
53% in Alberta
56% in Saskatchewan
50% in Manitoba

on an average day...

65% in Ontario
55% in Quebec
51% in New Brunswick
61% in Nova Scotia
49% in Prince Edward Island
39% in Newfoundland

Parking woes...

... The cost of tagging and towing cars is:

	Parking Ticket	Towing Charge	Total
Toronto	$40	$92	$132
Calgary	$30	$64.65	$94.65
Montreal	$40	$35	$75
Halifax	$15	$50	$65
Vancouver	$25	$16.25	$41.25

on an average day...

... 7,200 parking tickets are written in the City of Toronto

Of the total,

> 4,608 are for parking in no parking zones
> 2,160 are for expired meters
> 432 are given to cars in no standing or no stopping areas

... 25% of people ignore their parking ticket, hoping the government will forget about them

... 60% simply pay up

... 15% challenge the ticket in court

... 166 cars are photographed by Calgary's lone photo radar camera. Since its inception, 39 fewer accidents occur daily

on an average day...

Ride the rails...

... VIA Rail's Silver and Blue service, on the refurbished 1955 train named The Canadian, takes three and a half days to travel from Toronto to Vancouver or Vancouver to Toronto. Each day of the trip, 6.8 kilograms of coffee are brewed, kitchen staff prepare over 1,143 meals and porters make up 400 beds

on an average day...

Water ways...

... 549 boats pass through the 43 locks on the Trent-Severn Waterway near Peterborough, Ontario

... From May to October, the four boats that take tourists on the Niagara River to view the falls close up make 22 round trips. The boats are named The Maid of the Mist — numbers I to IV

Heading south...

... 7,143 Canadians visit Myrtle Beach, South Carolina, on each day of the annual Can-Am Week held during spring break in March

on an average day...

... Between January and March, 1,133 Canadians travel to Jamaica

... 959 Canadians, staying overnight in Kentucky while en route to or from Florida, spend $63,013

On the wild side...

... 17 Canadians trek off to Kenya to take part in a safari

A piece of the action...

... 120,000 Canadians own a time-share property

on an average day...

Only in Canada...

... Senior citizens travelling to Florida for the winter take the following items from home that they can't get while in the United States:

over-the-counter painkillers with codeine (a prescription is necessary in the United States)
Coffee Crisp chocolate bars
Red Rose tea
salt and vinegar potato chips
Shreddies cereal
plug-in kettles (not available in the United States because of some electrical safety standard quirk)

on an average day...

... When Americans return to the United States after a holiday in Canada, they bring home the following:

Cuban cigars (illegal in the United States due to the trade embargo with Cuba)
Iranian rugs
replacement china pieces from Ashley's china shops
maple syrup
Canadian bacon
Canadian beer
stuffed and mounted moose heads
mounted game fish

CASHING IN

on an average day...

Cold hard cash...

... If all Canadian paper money were collected, it would
be worth a face value of $23 billion

... 2 million $1,000 bills are in circulation

... The Royal Canadian Mint produces 80 solid gold bars
worth $170,000 each, for a total daily production
worth almost $14 million

... 10,685 ounces of gold bullion are sold

... The Canadian Mint produces 2,304,658 foreign coins
and 25,753 trade dollars, medals and tokens

on an average day...

... The average Canadian has $15.35 worth of nickels, dimes and quarters squirrelled away at home

... The Royal Canadian Mint estimates that there are 10 billion pennies worth $100 million stashed away in piggy banks coast to coast. This represents a six-year supply of pennies out of circulation

... The average Canadian household has $24 worth of pennies hidden in jars, vases, cupboards or drawers

on an average day...

... Even though the $1 bill was retired from circulation in 1989, average Canadians have tucked away 165 million of the bills as mementos

... In Montreal, the counterfeiting capital of Canada, $3,836 in fake currency is recovered and another $68,493 is still in circulation; 50% of the phony bills are U.S. $100 notes

Forgotten funds...

... The Bank of Canada pays out $6,849 on dormant, long-forgotten accounts. Another million dormant accounts containing a total of $126.1 million remain untouched. Anyone can contact the Bank of Canada for a name search, free of charge, by calling (613) 782-8583

on an average day...

Stocking up...

... 90 million shares worth almost $1 billion are traded on the Toronto Stock Exchange. About 80% of all stocks traded in Canada go through the TSE

... Profits generated by all member firms of all Canadian stock exchanges total $720,548

Taking credit...

... There are 50 million credit cards in circulation
Of these,

24.4 million are either VISA or MasterCard
17.5 million are department store cards
3.4 million are gas cards
The remainder are issued by small retail shops, diner clubs, American Express and EnRoute

on an average day...

... At any given time, 25 million credit cards are being used by Canadians in Canada

... The average Canadian owns 3 credit cards

... Equifax Canada Incorporated, a national credit information service, receives 233 calls from consumers wanting to check their credit rating

on an average day...

... 52% of those seeking credit are denied on their first try. The top 10 reasons why credit is denied are:

no credit history
slow payment history
accounts in collection
bankruptcy
statement of claims
repossession
foreclosure/power of sale
no income
short job history
not at current residence long enough

When credit's due...

... The average Canadian debtor owes $15,500

on an average day...

Charitable Canadians...

... 21% of all individual charitable donations are made by citizens aged 70 and over. This group is also the most generous in amounts of money given

... $684,932 is donated by Canadians to overseas charities

... $9,315 is donated by Canadians to Save the Children Fund Canada

You can't win without a ticket...

... Pro-line, the Ontario government's sports lottery, adds $628,571 to its coffers

on an average day...

... The average lottery player has an income of $47,200;
15% have incomes below $20,000, 40% have incomes
over $50,000. Lottery players are split equally between
men and women

... When major lottery winners were asked about how
they were treated after winning, only 28% said they
were contacted by the media
... Of those who did speak to the press:

95% said they were treated respectfully
13% were asked to make a charitable donation

... When $1 million lottery winners are asked what they
did with their winnings:

90% put the money in the bank
66% gave some to family and friends
63% travelled
42% bought a new home
11% started their own business

on an average day...

... William Hill, a bookmaking firm in London, England, puts the odds of Elvis Presley crash-landing his U.F.O. into Loch Ness, hitting Nessie (the Loch Ness Monster) in the process, at 14,000,000 to 1. Curiously, these are the same odds as winning Canada's 649 jackpot

Win, place or show?...

... Canadians bet $40 million on horse races

... $800,000 is wagered by telephone from Canada to Hong Kong bookmakers on Hong Kong horse races

on an average day...

Under the "B"...

... In Ontario, the bingo capital of North America, $4,109,589 is spent in bingo halls, church basements and other venues across the province

... 23,562 Albertans play bingo and spend an average of $29.65 each

... 11,415 Saskatchewaners play bingo, paying out an average of $28.65 each

... A bingo hall in Saskatchewan makes $274 by providing day-care services for bingo-playing parents

... The same bingo hall takes in $165 from the sale of ink dabbers, used by players to mark off called numbers

on an average day...

... Women bingo players outnumber men 4 to 1; most smoke and are over age 50

Casino Royale, Canadian style...

... The costs of gambling in Canada's 5 casinos are the following:

	Parking	Meal	Drink	Slot	Min. bet	Max. bet
Casino Windsor	$8	$15	$2-$3	.25	$15-$25	$5,000
Crystal Casino, Winnipeg	$4	$15	$3*	.05	$1	$500
Casino de Montréal	Free	$20	$3.25	.25	$1	$1,000
Vancouver Casino	Free	$10	$1.25*	n/a**	$1	$25
Emerald Casino, Saskatoon	Free	$10	$3.50	.25	$1.50	$100

* facilities not licensed

**slot machines are illegal in British Columbia

on an average day...

What it costs...

... A person living in an average poor urban family (annual family income of less than $25,000) spends $14.60

Of this amount,

$7.16 is spent on shelter
$4.75 is spent on food
$1.22 is spent on clothing
$1.47 is spent on other needs

... Every time a 747 takes off from Vancouver's airport, it costs $61,850

This price tag includes:

$35,000 for fuel
$9,100 for in-flight catering
$7,600 in fuel taxes
$4,000 for cleaning and ground handling
$3,240 for hotel accommodation and food for the
20-member crew
$1,990 landing fee
$920 terminal fee

on an average day...

... It costs $19,215 to record your own CD

Of the total,

$10,000 pays for studio time
$5,000 covers production fees
$2,790 pays for manufacturing and distribution
$1,175 is for liner notes and design
$250 is for tape mastering

Keeping up with the Joneses...

... It costs $31,650 to install an upscale wine cellar in your home:

$15,000 for construction (labour)
$12,000 for redwood tracking
$1,500 for a cooling system
$1,000 for French doors
$1,000 for a redwood tasting table
$750 for a temperature alarm
$400 for an inventory system

on an average day...

... It costs $20,600 to install an in-ground swimming pool
... It costs $20,000 to have a woodland style garden created
... It costs $17,000 to install a backyard tennis court
... It costs $10,000 to install a backyard waterfall and fountain
... It costs $9,000 for a custom-made backyard gazebo
... It costs $4,000 to have lighting installed in the backyard to create nightscaping
... It costs $3,000 to install a backyard fish pond

on an average day...

Phantom pricing...

... Each person visiting Toronto to see a performance of *The Phantom of the Opera* spends an average of $158.64

How visitors spend their money:

$70.00 on *Phantom* tickets
$38.64 on accommodation
$21.03 on souvenirs
$19.05 on restaurants
$6.07 on public transportation
$2.67 on private transportation
$1.18 on groceries

BUSINESS CONCERNS

on an average day...

Making it big...

... Lawrence Bloomberg, president and CEO of the investment firm First Marathon Inc., earns no salary but receives $18,904 in bonuses. He is the highest paid executive at any public company

... Raymond Cyr, chairman of Bell Canada and former chairman of BCE, makes $2,135 in salary and bonuses

... At Canada's largest corporation, BCE Inc., the company president and CEO collects $2,054 in salary and bonuses

... The CEO of Spar Aerospace, Canada's largest space company, is paid $1,575 in salary and bonuses

on an average day...

... The head of Coca-Cola Beverages Ltd. of Canada, William Casey, earns $1,096 in salary and $458 in bonuses

... At Canada's chartered banks:

	Income of CEO	Profits	Bad Loans/Debts
Bank of Montreal	$4,932	$1,942,466	$1,849,315
Canadian Imperial Bank of Commerce	$1,918	$2,000,000	$1,273,973
National Bank	$1,340	$479,452	$890,411
Royal Bank	$2,830	$821,918	$4,794,512
Scotia Bank	$2,411	$1,273,973	$1,956,164
Toronto Dominion	$4,178	$753,425	$1,643,836

... 55 copies of the Bank of Montreal's task force report to employees on the advancement of women in the bank are sent — on request — to organizations around the world. The report has attracted international attention and awards

on an average day...

Hidden agendas...

... Executives spend 52 minutes looking for things that
are misplaced, mislabelled
or misfiled

It's all in the name...

... 2,900 Canadian companies have the word "Royal" in
their name
... 2,100 businesses use "Dominion"
... 1,400 include the word "Imperial"
... 1,100 use "Crown"

on an average day...

Promotional perks...

... Companies spend $2,739,726 on keychains, pens, mugs and other items with their company logo printed on them. The promotional and motivational industry is one of the fastest growing in Canada

... Condom Sense/A Safe Investment sells 392 custom-ordered condoms wrapped in packets advertising company graphics and slogans

The price of ownership...

... To buy each of the following franchises, you would pay:

$122,141,500 for a major league baseball team
$109,284,500 for a National Basketball Association team
$64,285,000 for a National Hockey League team
$3,000,000 for a Canadian Football League team
$75,000 for a Swiss Chalet outlet

on an average day...

$50,000 for a Harvey's
$40,000 for a Burger King
$22,500 for a McDonald's
$20,000 for a Pizza Pizza
$10,000 for a Subway Sandwich store

Ode to Big Brother...

... The collection, compilation and sale of personal data nets $821,918

Modern marketing...

... $21,369,863 worth of products are bought by Canadians responding to direct marketing schemes on the radio, on television or in print ads. Canada Post earns 25% of its revenue by delivering these items

on an average day...

... 2 complaints are received by the Canadian Direct Marketing Association, usually for non-delivery of goods

... The Zellers Club Z program, in which regular shoppers earn points towards free merchandise, has 7 million members out of a possible 11 million Canadian households

Today's special is...

... Liquidation World, a chain of 12 stores across the country, employs 180 people, serves 8,219 customers and takes in $68,493 in sales. Its merchandise changes daily; Monday stores may have 10,000 canned hams, and Tuesday they may offer toilets at an irresistible price

on an average day...

You say potato and I say potatoe...

... New York Fries, a chain of specialty shops across
   Canada, uses 52,055 potatoes to make their unique
   fries

Rocky Mountain groceries...

... 4,000 customers use The Grocery Store in Whistler, B.C.
   During peak season, the store can turn over a quarter
   of its inventory in a single day, or about $50,000 worth
   of groceries

Small but mighty...

... British Columbia's 50 or so small publishers generate
   $54,795

on an average day...

... The New Age Publishing and Retailing Alliance, based on Orcas Island off Vancouver, has sales of $2,739,726

Something fowl...

... There are 400 ostrich ranchers in Canada. Ostrich meat sells for $40 a kilogram; a full-grown bird weighs more than 200 kilos

on an average day...

Ostrich and Peanut Butter Stew
1/4 cup peanut oil
0.9 kilograms (2 lbs) ostrich meat, diced
1 large onion, chopped
2 tomatoes, peeled and chopped
1 tablespoon tomato paste
2 1/2 cups boiling water
3/4 cup peanut butter
1 teaspoon crushed peppercorns
salt to taste
2 carrots, peeled and sliced
1 small eggplant, cubed
2 potatoes, peeled and cubed
half small cabbage, sliced
half 300-g package of frozen okra

Heat oil in large pan and sauté ostrich meat until browned. Remove meat and set aside. Add onions and cook for a few minutes to soften. Stir in tomatoes and tomato paste. Return ostrich to pan. Pour in water and add peanut butter. Season with salt and peppercorns. Stir well. Reduce heat and simmer 20 minutes. Check to see that the sauce is not sticking to bottom of pan. If necessary, add more water. Add carrots and eggplant; continue to cook for 10 minutes. Stir in potatoes and cabbage; cook for a further 15 minutes until spuds are tender. Add okra and simmer another five minutes.

on an average day...

Oh, nuts!...

... 1,085 kilograms of hazelnuts are grown on Tony Van den Brink's 180-acre orchard near Chilliwack, B.C. Most of the nuts are sold between Thanksgiving and Christmas. At Thanksgiving, Van den Brink allows families to collect their own nuts for 35 cents a pound

Creative Canadians...

... 3 original Canadian products are assessed by the Canadian Industrial Innovation Centre, an offshoot of the University of Waterloo, for potential marketability

... 10,000 Canadians are busy designing everything from yachts to sleeping bags, movie sets to computer software

on an average day...

... 57 patents are issued

... One day a month, Canada Games holds "Game Day,"
   when would-be game creators get to make their pitch;
   if successful, they will sell the rights to their ideas

Non-profit ventures...

... 80,000 not-for-profit associations operate in Canada

Spreading the word...

... Photocopiers use 9,589 toner cartridges, 25% of which
   are recycled

---

on an average day...

... The 19 photocopiers at Cantel Incorporated's head office produce 15,000 copies

... An average large company in Canada spends $5,479 on faxes

... Canada's 1 million fax machines receive 5 million "junk faxes," which use up 300 tonnes of paper — the equivalent of 4,110 trees

Parcel post...

... The cost of sending a 2.2 kilogram package, first class:

Vancouver to Tokyo	$51.90
Tokyo to Vancouver	$55.94
Toronto to London, England	$33.90
London, England, to Toronto	$31.71

on an average day...

Montreal to Paris	$33.90
Paris to Montreal	$62.76
Halifax to Melbourne	$51.90
Melbourne to Halifax	$43.65

... Canada's direct mail marketers put 42,191,780 flyers and coupons under our doors and in our mailboxes

... 2,191,781 definitive Canadian Maple Leaf 43-cent stamps are printed by Australian printing giant Leigh-Mardon Proprietary Ltd. The company also prints the $1 and $2 definitive stamps in Canada Post's architectural series

---

on an average day...

You called?...

... 11 million households have at least one cordless telephone

... 300,000 Canadians shun high tech and still rely on telephone party lines

... 800,000 Canadians carry a pager. Of these, 240,000 are to receive personal calls

... Canadians leave 32,876,712 voice-mail messages — an average of more than one message for every man, woman and child in the country

---

on an average day...

We've got your number...

... Since call-display has become available, the number of obscene phone calls investigated by police in Toronto has fallen from 11 to 2

The hardware...

... 2.4 million households in Canada have a computer; 500,000 also have a modem

... 548 people buy a notebook computer

... Computer ownership by province:

43% in British Columbia
49% in Alberta
34% in Saskatchewan

on an average day...

29% in Manitoba
45% in Ontario
33% in Quebec
17% in New Brunswick
27% in Nova Scotia
13% in Prince Edward Island
23% in Newfoundland

... Percentage who think owning a computer is essential, by region:

26% in British Columbia
31% in the Prairie provinces
28% in Ontario
15% in Quebec
24% in the Atlantic provinces

... When asked, "Who in your family uses the computer most frequently?":

43% say the person who purchased it
29% say another adult in the household
19% say children under 18 years of age
9% say it is equally shared by the family

on an average day...

... Of the 4 million personal computers owned by Canadians, 3 million are owned by people who really don't know how to use them except for basic word processing

The software...

... MaranGraphics, a Mississauga-based company, sells 639 copies of comic books designed to take computer weenies through step-by-step explanations of popular software programs

on an average day...

... Of Canadians who own a personal computer:

88% own word processing software
72% own games software
66% own spreadsheet/financial software
45% own a modem
27% own a CD-ROM

... Bankware, distributed free by the CIBC to its customers, is the only comprehensive banking software on the market. It provides users with mortgage amortization charts, calculates the probability of approval for loan applications and structures entire personal budgets

The information superhighway...

... 300,000 Canadians are members of Internet, a superhighway of telephone lines that link up 30 million computers and their users around the world

---

on an average day...

... 25,000 Canadians use the country's two largest computer networks: the Toronto-based CRS On-Line and the Ottawa-based National Capital Free Net

... The words "information superhighway" appear twice in *The Globe and Mail*, Canada's National Newspaper

Gizmos and gadgets...

... We buy 633 camcorders

... 81% of Canadians use their VCR at least once to record a television program to watch at a later time

on an average day...

Snap stats...

... Japan Camera franchises across Canada develop 178,082 photographs

... 3,562 cameras are purchased, most of which are the instamatic point-and-shoot variety

MARKETING
COMMODITIES

on an average day...

All the best from Canada...

... Canada's 100,000 beef cattle producers bring in $4,109,589; they export 44% of their total production

... 233 horses in Canada are slaughtered to satisfy the foreign appetite for horsemeat

Of the total horsemeat exports,

20,000 kilograms are shipped to France
12,055 kilograms are shipped to Japan
6,027 kilograms are shipped to Italy
3,562 kilograms are shipped to Belgium

... 46,575 tonnes of wheat are exported. Canada's top customers are China, South Korea and the United States

on an average day...

... 24,657 kilograms of Ontario tobacco are exported to major U.S. markets

... $136,986 worth of Canadian-grown ginseng is exported

... Canada exports $8,219,178 worth of lumber to the United States
... 80% of this lumber comes from the forests of British Columbia
... Canada provides the United States with 27% of all its lumber needs

... $191,781 worth of fur garments are exported. Of the total, 80% are shipped to the United States

---

on an average day...

... 1,096 men's wool suits are exported to the United States under the free trade agreement

... 20 tonnes of clean, wearable old clothes are sorted at the Goodwill Industries Toronto plant. The clothes, which could not be sold at Goodwill thrift stores, are shipped to developing countries

... Uganda, Zaire and Ghana are the top 3 importers of Canadian used clothing

... Canada ships $621,918 worth of military goods to Saudi Arabia, including $594,520 worth of vehicles

on an average day...

... **$205,479** worth of Canadian television shows are
exported
... The top 5 export countries are:

United States
France
United Kingdom
Germany
Italy

... Kevin Sullivan's production of *Anne of Green Gables*,
the number 1 Canadian TV export, is available in 84
countries around the world

on an average day...

... Other Canadian television shows available abroad
   include:

   Road to Avonlea (72 countries)
   Neon Rider (65)
   E.N.G. (48)
   Street Legal (32)
   The Red Green Show (30) (this program is Turkey's
   favourite television import)

... Grace Hospital in Vancouver (the largest birth centre
   in Canada) earns $6.85 on sales of placentas to a cos-
   metics lab in France. The money collected goes into a
   nursing education fund

on an average day...

From abroad...

... Canada imports 159 tonnes of Australian boneless beef. The lower-quality beef is used to make ground beef products

... We import 75,616,000 kilograms of tomato paste from California, worth $54,795

... Duchy Original biscuits, produced by the farms of HRH Prince Charles, are sold exclusively in Canada by Holt Renfrew & Co. Ltd. A box of 20 oat biscuits or 16 ginger cookies retails for $6.50. Profits from the sales are donated to British charities

... Canadians buy $164,384 worth of Oriental and Persian rugs

on an average day...

... We import 822 Russian-made hockey sticks

... Canada imports $1,698,630 worth of books from the
   United States

... Canada imports $180,822 worth of books from France
... France, however, imports only $41,096 worth of
   Canadian books

GOVERNING
THOUGHTS

on an average day...

The debt...

... The federal government goes $100 million further into
debt

A taxing situation...

... 340 of the 37,310 Canadians earning over $250,000 do
not pay any income taxes
... 2,000 Canadians earning over $100,000 do not pay
income taxes
... 8,360 Canadians earning over $50,000 do not pay
income taxes

... 30 tips to Revenue Canada are made by Canadians
tattling on friends, relatives and colleagues who they
suspect are cheating on their taxes. Of these 30 tips,
1 leads to a prosecution

---

on an average day...

... 53,973 Canadians file their
income taxes

Of the total,

12,329 have mistakes
1,205 are filed electronically
33,151 of them will get refunds
averaging $924 each
8,712 will pay the government
an average of $2,107

... The others may have money
coming to them but they won't
see it because they owe back taxes
or other monies to Revenue
Canada

... 200 people have their tax returns audited by Revenue
Canada; another 3,288 are partially audited.
Altogether, the audits bring in an additional
$9,589,041 from the pockets of taxpayers

... The federal government collects $40,921,917 from the GST

on an average day...

... Canada Customs inspectors rake in $432,876,712 in taxes and duties at 130 land border crossings, 172 airports and 255 commercial importation sites

... Canada ties Norway in paying the highest beer taxes in the world — about 53% of total cost. Spain has the lowest beer taxes at 10% of total cost

Type	Fed. Tax	Average Prov. Tax
24 bottles of domestic	$3.70	$5.33
24 cans of domestic	$4.09	$5.53
24 bottles of imported	$4.15	$5.76
24 cans of imported	$4.11	$7.90

Parliamentary gems...

... Members of Parliament receive $521 each to run their offices

on an average day...

... The Speaker of the House has $1,611 to spend on entertainment, and shares a travel budget of $1,901 with the Speaker of the Senate

... The federal government spends $1,736 to have the official shredder at the National Archives shred classified documents into 19 tonnes of paper tinsel. If the shelves of documents being shredded were placed side by side, they would stretch for 23 kilometres

... Canadian taxpayers pay $6,301 to subsidize eating establishments on Parliament Hill. A typical lunch of a hamburger, fries, large drink and dessert at the subsidized cafeterias and canteens costs $4.50

on an average day...

... Upon retirement from the House of Commons, Members of Parliament can buy their green chairs for $900. Less than 2% do

Women in the House...

... Women make up 18% of the House of Commons

... The percentage of women in the provincial and territorial legislatures:

25% in British Columbia
19% in Alberta
18% in Saskatchewan
21% in Manitoba
21% in Ontario
18% in Quebec
17% in New Brunswick
10% in Nova Scotia

on an average day...

25% in Prince Edward Island
6% in Newfoundland
8% in the Northwest Territories
19% in the Yukon Territory

Social security...

... A Canadian on social security benefits receives $5.81
... In comparison, a person on social security would be
given:

$13.44 in Sweden
$10.49 in France
$5.72 in the United States
$0.05 in Mexico

... The federal government pays out $602,740 in pensions
to people who are not eligible

on an average day...

Money well spent?...

... In the Public Accounts of Canada, there is a list over 100 pages long of groups and organizations that receive money from the federal government. The grants range from less than $10,000 to more than $17 million. A typical day's worth of grants could include:

Fur Institute of Canada	$390,000
Canadian Association of Police Chiefs	$49,000
Consumers Association of Canada	$800,631
International Federation of Library Associations	$11,000
Canadian Labour Congress	$4,193,100
Planned Parenthood Federation of Canada	$146,000
National Action Committee on the Status of Women	$300,000
Canadian Association of Broadcasters	$216,400
Canadian Table Tennis Association	$444,697

on an average day...

Inquiring minds want to know...

... 20 requests for information are made under the Access
to Information Act
... 21 complaints are lodged by citizens unable to get
information they wanted
... 1 person takes Federal Court action to get information

Free trade...

... As a result of the Free Trade Agreement, 247,558
Americans are employed by Canadian manufacturing
firms across the United States; each American
employee earns an average of $69.73 (U.S.) a day
... Michigan has 122 Canadian firms employing 8,300
people
... New York State has 171 Canadian firms employing
56,900 workers
... Kentucky has 14 Canadian-owned companies employing 2,334 people

on an average day...

Our favourite topic...

... Environment Canada weather services across the country cost each Canadian 2 cents

Keeping the peace...

... 73,000 Canadians are members of the active military forces
... 30,000 belong to the military reserves

... 3,317 Canadians are involved in military peacekeeping missions around the world

... In December 1994, Operation Santa Claus, organized by soldiers' wives in Petawawa, sent 3,301 Christmas stockings to Canadian peacekeepers overseas

CRIME AND
PUNISHMENT

on an average day...

At risk...

... When Canadians are asked, "Have you, a family member or a close friend been a victim of crime?":

67% say no
13% say they, personally, have been a victim of crime
12% say a family member has been a victim
5% say a close friend has been a victim
3% say yes to a combination of the three options

... Percentage who report being a victim of crime, by province:

43% in British Columbia
42% in Alberta
33% in Saskatchewan
38% in Manitoba
37% in Ontario
21% in Quebec
18% in New Brunswick
21% in Nova Scotia
25% in Prince Edward Island
19% in Newfoundland

on an average day...

Violent charges...

... 301 men are charged with violent crimes
... 36 women are charged with violent crimes

... Canadians give the following reasons for the increase in violent crime:

40% say the justice system is too lenient
20% say parents fail to pass on the right values to their children
12% blame violence on television
6% blame our immigration policies
5% blame the absence of stronger gun-control laws
13% cite all of the above
4% cite other reasons

... 10% of Quebeckers believe the absence of stronger gun controls is the main reason for the increase in violent crime; only 1% of Canadians living in Western Canada agree

on an average day...

Armed and dangerous...

... Canadians own 7 million legal firearms — 6 million rifles and shotguns, and 1 million handguns, machine guns, antique and collector's guns

... 152 new restricted weapons are registered with the police

... In total, 1.2 million restricted weapons are registered with the RCMP; 900,000 Canadians own a permit for these weapons

... 8 legally registered guns are stolen

on an average day...

... 66% of Canadians favour a ban on handguns; 36% of Americans agree

... 56% of Canadians believe citizens have a right to own a gun; 86% of Americans feel the same way

... 34% of Canadian households own a firearm; in the United States, 46% of households own a firearm

... 461 guns were surrendered to police during each of the 45 days of the 1993 firearms amnesty; 189 other firearms, such as explosives, grenades and military shells, were also turned in on each of those days

To serve and protect...

... When Canadians are asked, "In bringing criminals to justice, how should the police behave?":

61% say police should abide by all laws
23% say police should bend some laws to catch criminals
16% say police should break the law, if necessary

---

on an average day...

... The provincial breakdown of those who say police
should break the law, if necessary, is as follows:

4% in British Columbia
10% in Alberta
10% in Saskatchewan
4% in Manitoba
13% in Ontario
29% in Quebec
20% in New Brunswick
17% in Nova Scotia
11% in Prince Edward Island
11% in Newfoundland

... 3 officers on the Metro Toronto police force draw their
gun
... In Edmonton, a city with 616,700 residents compared
with Metro Toronto's 2,275,000, 2 officers draw their gun

... 63 Canadians are enrolled in the ultra-secret RCMP
witness-protection program. The program costs taxpayers $3,014 to operate

on an average day...

... Police in Metro Toronto answer 548 alarms from
private home
security systems
... 98% are false
alarms

The case for DNA...

... DNA figures in the evidence of 1 Canadian trial

on an average day...

Do the crime...

... Canada Customs makes 79 seizures of liquor and cigarettes, as well as 23 seizures of pornographic goods, 5 seizures of weapons and 6 seizures of drugs

... Canada is a major money-laundering centre, with $32,876,712 (U.S.) in drug-related money passing through financial institutions

... 1 incident of anti-Semitic vandalism or harassment is reported

... 5 prostitutes and 3 of their customers are arrested in Montreal

on an average day...

... It costs $685 to support a heroin addiction
... A heroin addict costs society $2,740
... There are an estimated 20,000 addicts in Metro
Toronto alone

Do the time...

... It costs Canadian taxpayers $183.56 to keep an inmate
in a maximum security prison, $120.55 in medium
security and $90.41 in minimum security

... 4,110 licence plates are
produced by inmates at
Millbrook Correctional
Centre near
Peterborough. Each
inmate, paid $2.00 a
day for this work, can spend
his money in the canteen

on an average day...

... 30 guards supervise 5 prisoners residing at Canadian Forces Service Prison & Detention Centre, Canada's only military prison. The longest any prisoner stays is two years, and then he or she is transferred to a regular federal penitentiary

Leaving on a jet plane...

... 25 people are deported from Canada

... 26,000 orders for deportation are outstanding

on an average day...

Silence is frozen...

... In Vancouver, the amplified sound system that heralds
the arrival of an ice cream truck has been banned
through a new city ordinance. Says anti-chime
Councillor Gordon Price, "How many times can you
hear, 'Turkey in the Straw'?"

OUR GREAT LAND

on an average day...

Abusing our country...

... 71,233 tires are scrapped:

8,671 are thrown away in British Columbia
6,849 in Alberta
3,740 in Saskatchewan
2,740 in Manitoba
23,603 in Ontario
18,434 in Quebec
1,918 in New Brunswick
3,466 in Nova Scotia
274 in Prince Edward Island
1,538 in Newfoundland

... Of the total tires scrapped
across the country:

35,178 end up in landfills
10,959 are exported
9,205 are stockpiled
6,137 are recycled
5,644 go to
unknown
destinations
4,110 are burned
as fuel

on an average day...

... 91,151 oil filters end up in landfills across the country; from these filters, 32,877 litres of benzene and arsenic-laced oil leach into the earth

... 35,616 of these oil filters are thrown away by Ontario drivers

... Halifax and its sister city, Dartmouth, pour 100 million litres of raw sewage into Halifax harbour

... 90.8 million litres of raw sewage are dumped into the waters surrounding Victoria, B.C. The city, which takes in $2,054,795 from tourism, is beginning to suffer from ill winds, so to speak

... 500 billion litres of raw sewage — the equivalent of 32 Exxon-Valdez supertanker loads — are dumped into Canadian waterways, according to a survey of 20 sewage-treatment systems across Canada conducted by the Vancouver-based Sierra Legal Defence Fund

on an average day...

... 822 people are made ill as a result of their environment

... Health and Welfare Canada acknowledges that there are 11,000 known contaminated sites, 1,000 of which pose significant health or environmental risk — yet most of us are unaware of their locations

... In Saint John, N.B., garbage collectors wrestle 50,000 kilograms of garbage each spring day, 14,286 kilograms more than at any other time of the year

... 63% of households with children aged two and under use disposable diapers exclusively
... 43% of babies in British Columbia wear disposable diapers, the lowest percentage in the country
... 77% of babies in Newfoundland wear disposable diapers exclusively, the highest percentage in Canada

on an average day...

Waste not, want not...

... 5,760 acres of Canadian wilderness are lost to environmental and human exploitation

... 342,466 styrofoam coffee cups are recycled by The Canadian Polystyrene Recycling Association into 38,356,164 pellets of resin; these pellets are used to make office products and audio cassettes

... Toronto's Royal York Hotel uses a pulping machine to separate liquid from food waste; the dry product is sold as livestock feed instead of being shipped to landfill sites

... The hotel also recycles 273 kilograms of corrugated papers, saving 6 trees

on an average day...

... 35% of British Columbians compost regularly — this is more than double the national figure

Tree-huggers...

... Out of 10 million Canadian households, only 5,198,000 have access to paper recycling. Of those that do have a recycling program in their area, an estimated 4,462,000 use the service

... 95% of Ontarians recycle newspapers

on an average day...

... Of the 1,500 different magazines published in Canada, only 510 of them are printed on recycled paper

... The National Library in Ottawa treats 55 books for damage caused by acidic paper, at a cost of approximately $10 per book

... 45% of Canadians buy paper products made with recycled materials

... 43,836 cubic metres of plant and tree life in British Columbia are destroyed by insects and disease. The worst culprit is the dwarf mistletoe, a parasitic plant that accounts for more than a third of the total loss

on an average day...

... An average-sized tree grown in Canada will produce 453,000 toothpicks

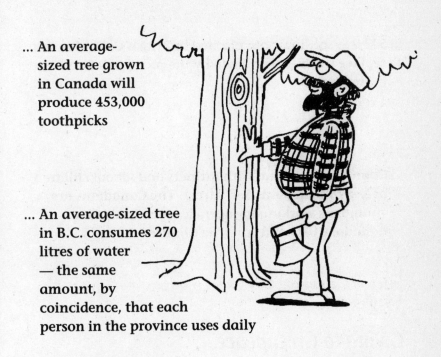

... An average-sized tree in B.C. consumes 270 litres of water — the same amount, by coincidence, that each person in the province uses daily

... 10,411 trees are planted by Scouts Canada, with the help of the National Community Tree Foundation and Tree Plan Canada

on an average day...

... 547,945 seedlings are planted in British Columbia to replace the trees cut down by the province's forest industries

... Canadians working with farmers and school children in Kenya help plant 5,479 trees. The Canadians are volunteers working for agencies such as Oxfam Canada, CUSO and Save the Children

Giving to Greenpeace...

... 896 Canadians donate money to Greenpeace Canada. As Greenpeace is not a registered charity, donations are not tax-deductible. However, the organization also runs Greenpeace Canada Charitable Foundation, a certified charity that funds non-adversarial research

---

on an average day...

How cold was it?...

... Thanks to the breakup of the Soviet Union, Russia is
now the coldest country year-round, with an average
temperature of -5.3°C. Canada is second, with an average temperature of -4.4°C
... The warmest province is Nova Scotia, with an average
temperature of 6.2°C

CELEBRATIONS

on an average day...

Lighten Up Canada Day...

... 125,000 red foam noses are sold throughout Central Ontario on the first Monday in February for the annual Lighten Up Canada Day, a day of fun and frolic

... The residents of Acton, Ontario, who wear red noses to celebrate their annual Lighten Up Canada Day, are listed in the Guinness Book of World Records as having the longest continuous line of people wearing red noses: 1,588

on an average day...

Will you be my Valentine?...

... Canadians send 20 million Valentines

... 69,494 wire orders for flowers are placed for Valentine's Day

... A perfect Valentine's Day costs about $450:

$1.88 for the card
$13.56 for a pound of chocolates
$37.66 for a dozen roses
$112.99 for dinner and dancing
$263.63 for limo rental
$12.81 for a night cap at a club with a view

... The same perfect Valentine's Day costs:

$1,300 in Tokyo
$950 in Paris
$320 in Athens
$300 in Sydney

---

on an average day...

Coloured eggs and chocolate bunnies...

... Canadians send 15 million Easter cards

... 21,657 wire orders for flowers are placed for Easter

... 320,104 long distance calls are made by Canadians on Easter Sunday

Just for Moms...

... Canadians send 17 million Mother's Day cards

on an average day...

... 74,489 wire orders for flowers are placed for Mother's Day

... 390,008 long distance phone calls are made on Mother's Day

... On Mother's Day, Bell Canada receives 12,000 calls to directory assistance from people requesting their mother's phone number

A day for Dads...

... Canadians send 11 million Father's Day cards

on an average day...

... 2,215 wire orders for Father's Day flowers are placed

... 396,428 long distance calls are made on Father's Day

Thanks for giving...

... 334,048 long distance calls are made on Thanksgiving Day

A day to remember...

... 2 million poppies are sold by Canadian Veterans each day of the week leading up to Remembrance Day on November 11

on an average day...

... At the 1994 Remembrance Day luncheon hosted by the National Press Club, the guests ate 360 kilograms of Hormel Foods Corporation's "Spam," which became a staple of Allied diets during World War II. Brits and Canadians would trade rum and cigarettes for the little tins of meat

Deck the halls...

... 1.5 million live trees are decked with tinsel and ornaments in homes across the country
... Another 1.5 million trees are exported to the United States for decorating

... The Christmas tree industry makes $150,685

on an average day...

... By Christmas Day, 110 million Christmas cards have been exchanged within Canada

... Canadians send 35 million Christmas cards through the mail on each of the 10 days before Christmas

... Canada Post receives 80,000 letters addressed to Santa Claus each day for the 10 days leading up to Christmas. About 8,000 Canada Post volunteers help Santa answer his mail

---

on an average day...

... 83,022 wire orders for flowers are placed for Christmas

... 433,639 long distance calls are made by Canadians on Christmas Day

... At Christmastime:

85% of Canadians put up a Christmas tree
77% have a turkey dinner
55% go to church
57% hang stockings
47% have a nativity scene in their home

... In the last week before Christmas, the average person spends 10 minutes a day bickering with someone over which parties to attend, what to wear and whether to leave early

on an average day...

... It would cost $22,036.49 to buy all the gifts listed in the carol "The Twelve Days of Christmas":

partridge in a pear tree ($20.73 for the partridge, $27.62 for the pear tree)	$48.35
2 turtle doves	$69.11
3 French hens	$20.73
4 calling birds	$386.99
5 gold rings (plain gold wedding bands)	$621.95
6 geese a-laying	$207.32
7 swans a-swimming	$9,674.70
8 maids a-milking (for an hour at minimum wage)	$46.99
9 ladies dancing	$3,602.90
10 lords a-leaping	$4,163.76
11 pipers piping	$1,532.97
12 drummers drumming	$1,660.72

PARTRIDGE
IN A PEAR TREE
$48.35

on an average day...

... On December 25, 1994, Bell Canada gave their cellular
   phone customers a special Christmas gift: free calls all
   day long
... 751,174 calls were made, allowing over 1.5 million
   people to exchange holiday wishes

WHERE WE BELONG

on an average day...

Join the club...

... There are about 90 winemaking clubs in Canada, each with approximately 30 members. Half of these groups are in Ontario and a quarter of them are in British Columbia

... 40,000 Canadians are members of Coupon Clippers, a coupon-exchange club. To become a member, write to: Coupon Clippers of Canada, 6554 Harmony Avenue, Niagara Falls, Ontario, L2H 1Z4

... 100,000 Canadians are members of IKEA's Family Club. After paying an annual fee, they are entitled to special prices and are given one evening's headstart on the annual summer sale

on an average day...

Brain strain...

... 3,000 Canadians belong to Mensa, a group whose members have an IQ higher than 98% of the population. To be considered a candidate, an applicant must have an IQ of at least 135

Happy campers...

... From July 28 to August 1, Canadians can boldly go where few have gone before — Klingon Language Camp at Bird's Hill Provincial Park, 60 km north of Winnipeg. For $315, excluding meals, campers receive 32 hours of classroom instruction in piQad, the Klingon alphabet and number system

on an average day...

Swat team...

... 37 Canadians are members of the World Flyswatting Federation. Their goal is to take flyswatting from underneath the kitchen sink and to establish it as a bona fide demonstration event at the first Summer Olympics of the 21st century

Out of context...

... 220 Canadians are members of The Society for Creative Anachronism

on an average day...

A second look...

... 800 Canadians belong to the National Leather Association, which includes fans of fetishism, aficionados of sadomasochism and other slaves of leather fashion — slave being the operative word

... 151 men belong to the Canadian Cross Dressers Club

Not what it seems...

... 300 Canadian families belong to the False Memory Syndrome Foundation, a support group for both innocent families accused of abuse and for survivors of abuse who are disbelieved by society

on an average day...

Pay up...

... 3 lawyers are suspended by the Law Society of Upper
Canada for not paying their annual membership fees

OPINIONATED

on an average day...

Our national identity...

... When Canadians are asked, "Do you think of yourself as a Canadian first, or as a resident of a particular region or province?":

72% say Canadian
22% say
provincial
resident
6% say regional
resident

... When asked, "Overall, how do you tend to view Canada today: as a pact between two founding groups, French and English, or as a relationship among ten equal provinces?":

49% say two founding groups
46% say ten equal provinces
5% have no opinion

on an average day...

... When asked, "Would you be sad/heartbroken if
Quebec were to separate from the rest of Canada?":

48% of those in Quebec said yes
64% of Canadians outside of Quebec said yes

... When asked, "Do you think Canada is the best country in the world in which to live?":

91% agree
9% disagree

... 83% of respondents in Quebec agree

... When asked, "Do you think, over the past decade, that
Canada has become a better place to live, a worse
place to live, or no better or worse?":

42% say no better or worse
39% say worse
19% say better

on an average day...

Our regional identity...

... When asked, "Given a choice, which province would you live in?":

27% say British Columbia
26% say Ontario
21% say Quebec
12% say Alberta
4% say Nova Scotia
3% say Manitoba
2% say Saskatchewan
2% say New Brunswick
2% say Newfoundland
1% say Prince Edward Island

All our worries...

... When asked, "What are the most important problems facing Canada?":

36% say unemployment/the economy
26% say government spending/the deficit
6% say crime and violence

on an average day...

5% say taxes
4% say national unity
23% give other answers or say they don't know

... When young Canadians aged 12 to 17 are asked what their top 5 concerns are, they reply:

war and suffering
the environment
death
AIDS
racism

Brave new world...

... When Canadians are asked, "Will Canada become a cashless society in our lifetime?":

60% say yes
36% say no
4% don't know

on an average day...

Our neighbourhoods...

... When Canadians are asked, "Is there any area within a mile of where you live where you would be afraid to walk at night?":

36% say yes
63% say no
1% are unsure

... When the same question is asked of just women:

51% say yes
48% say no
1% are unsure

... Women, by region,	Yes	No	Unsure
British Columbia	62%	38%	
Prairies	56%	43%	1%
Ontario	58%	41%	1%
Quebec	56%	43%	1%
Atlantic	31%	69%	

... Women, by age,	Yes	No	Unsure
18–29 years	56%	42%	2%
30–39 years	46%	53%	1%
40–49 years	40%	60%	
50–64 years	60%	40%	
65 years and over	67%	32%	1%

on an average day...

... 74% of Canadians are against the sale of beer and wine in neighbourhood corner stores

Believing what we read and hear...

... 81% of Canadians say television is the most credible medium and is a good influence

... 71% of Canadians think that newspapers are credible and trustworthy

on an average day...

Religious conviction...

... 47% of Canadians think that organized religion can be trusted and is a good influence

It's tempting...

... When Canadians are asked what they would do if they received a cheque for $1,000 from the government that was obviously an error:

69% say they would send it back
26% would deposit the cheque and wait to see what happens
5% would cash the cheque and spend it as quickly as possible

... Percentage of those who would deposit or cash the cheque, by province:

29% in British Columbia
22% in Alberta
30% in Saskatchewan
27% in Manitoba
30% in Ontario

on an average day...

39% in Quebec
20% in New Brunswick
30% in Nova Scotia
19% in Prince Edward Island
8% in Newfoundland

Criminal ideas...

... When Canadians are asked, "Where do you place the blame for the increase in crime and vandalism in our cities?", the top 4 answers are:

lack of family values
too few limits on teens
society's indifference
both parents working outside the home

... When asked, "Do you believe prostitution should be legal?", 52% of Canadians agree
... By province:

57% agree in British Columbia

on an average day...

52% agree in Alberta
36% agree in Saskatchewan
42% agree in Manitoba
52% agree in Ontario
59% agree in Quebec
30% agree in New Brunswick
50% agree in Nova Scotia
30% agree in Prince Edward Island
25% agree in Newfoundland

Joking around...

... When we are asked about telling a racial or ethnic joke:

50% of Canadians say it is never okay
29% say sometimes okay
17% say usually not okay
2% say always okay
2% say okay as long as you don't get caught

on an average day...

Relating and relationships...

... 45% of Canadians believe the way to the heart is through the stomach

... 34% describe the aroma of bread baking as the "scent of seduction"

... 25% have used a good home-cooked meal to seduce a lover or spouse

... 20% say they'd rather have a home-cooked meal than have sex

... When Canadians are asked, "Do you support the custom of a woman taking her husband's name when she marries?", 33% of women and 61% of men say yes

An affair to remember...

... In Canada, 14% of married men and 7% of married women admit to having had an affair

on an average day...

... Percentage of men and women who admit to having had an affair, by province:

7% in British Columbia
12% in Alberta
8% in Saskatchewan
5% in Manitoba
9% in Ontario
16% in Quebec
10% in New Brunswick
7% in Nova Scotia
4% in Prince Edward Island
6% in Newfoundland

... When married Canadians are asked what they would do if someone expressed interest in having an affair with them:

89% say they would appreciate the interest shown, but would not have an affair
8% say they would have a quick affair and hope no one finds out
3% say they would have an affair with the hopes that it would turn into a longer relationship

on an average day...

... Percentage who say they would have an affair, by province:

6% in British Columbia
5% in Alberta
1% in Saskatchewan
7% in Manitoba
8% in Ontario
13% in Quebec
7% in New Brunswick
6% in Nova Scotia
3% in Prince Edward Island
4% in Newfoundland

Barbie loves Ken...

... When asked by Mattel Canada, 61% of Canadians feel that Barbie and Ken should continue their 30-year relationship

on an average day...

What a thought!...

... 80% of men wouldn't want to become pregnant, even if they could. The major reason cited? The pain of childbirth

Getting personal...

... When parents are asked to respond to the statement, "It would be fine if one of my children turned out to be gay":

10% strongly agree
41% agree
27% disagree
13% strongly disagree
9% have no answer

... When parents are asked, "Would it bother you if openly gay and lesbian teachers were teaching your children?":

on an average day...

13% strongly agree
26% agree
41% disagree
11% strongly disagree
9% have no opinion

... When Canadians are asked if pornographic material
is always degrading to women:

18% strongly agree
45% agree
26% disagree
3% strongly disagree
8% have no opinion

... When asked if watching an X-rated movie is accept-
able:

7% say it's always okay
41% say it's sometimes okay
13% say it's usually not okay
37% say it's never okay
2% say it's okay as long as you don't get caught

---

on an average day...

... When asked about smoking marijuana:

66% say it's never okay
16% say it's sometimes okay
10% say it's usually not okay
5% say it's okay as long as you don't get caught
3% say it is always okay

Let's talk about sex...

... When Canadians are asked, "How many times a month, on average, do you have sex?", the average national response is 7
... By province:

7 in British Columbia
8 in Alberta
5 in Saskatchewan
7 in Manitoba
6 in Ontario
8 in Quebec
6 in New Brunswick
6 in Nova Scotia
8 in Prince Edward Island
10 in Newfoundland

on an average day...

... When Canadians are asked to describe their sex lives:

  12% say they are very sexually active
  50% say they are somewhat sexually active
  17% say they are not very sexually active
  13% say they are not sexually active
  8% do not answer

... The average Canadian sexual encounter lasts 39 minutes

... When we are asked what Canadians' attitudes on sexual matters have become over the past 10 to 20 years:

  43% say they are far more permissive
  31% say they are somewhat more permissive
  11% say they are about the same
  10% say they are somewhat more conservative
  5% say they are far more conservative

on an average day...

... When asked, "How many sexual partners have you
had in the past year?":

15% say zero
69% say one
8% say two
5% say three or four
3% say five or more

... When asked if diseases such as AIDS have really
affected their sex life:

12% of Canadians strongly agree
27% agree
39% disagree
10% strongly disagree
12% have no opinion

... When asked how often they think about having sex
with a stranger:

52% of Canadians say never
19% say rarely
19% say sometimes

on an average day...

4% say often
6% have no answer

... 38% of men and 8% of women answer "sometimes" or "often"

... 68% of men like the way they look naked, while only 22% of women like the way they look without clothes

How we feel...

... When Canadians are asked, "What are your major health concerns?", the top 7 responses are:

cancer
heart/stroke
weight
stress
aging
AIDS
pain

---

on an average day...

... When we are asked, "When a person has an incurable disease that causes great suffering, do you think that competent doctors should be allowed by law to end the patient's life through mercy killing, if the patient has made a formal written request?":

77% say yes
17% say no
6% don't know

... By age:

	Yes	No	Don't Know
18–19 years	85%	11%	4%
30–39 years	79%	15%	6%
40–49 years	77%	19%	4%
50–64 years	70%	21%	9%
65 and over	70%	20%	10%

Hard at work...

... When asked, "Would you work fewer hours to save someone else's job?":

49% say yes
51% say no

on an average day...

... Of those who daydream at work:

94% say it promotes creativity

57% picture themselves solving their company's biggest problem

88% think about quitting their job to become a success at something totally different

80% of men and 51% of women fantasize about having sex with a co-worker

... At the end of the day, 46% of Canadians often feel that they have not accomplished what they set out to do that morning

on an average day...

Juicy trial...

... 37% of Canadians say they have changed their daily routine at least occasionally to watch the O.J. Simpson trial

... 5% admit to stopping their regular routine to watch it

... 13% of Canadian viewers find the trial educational, while the remainder watch the trial for entertainment. Viewership is equally divided between men and women

Would you lend your toothbrush?...

... 97% of Canadians say they would not borrow someone else's toothbrush if they had forgotten their own on an overnight trip

Final thoughts...

... 45% of Canadians often feel under stress when they don't have enough time

on an average day...

... 32% feel that they don't spend enough time with family or friends
... 25% consider themselves workaholics
... 21% plan to slow down in the coming year

Sources

PEOPLE AND PETS

Baby face...
p. 4, Toronto Star, August 20/94; p. 4, Canadian Grocer, May 1993; p. 4, Canadian Living, August 1993; p. 5, Globe and Mail, January 9/93; p. 5, Report on Business Magazine, November 1993; p. 6, Canadian Family Physician, April 1993; p. 6, Statistics Canada, The 1995 Canadian Global Almanac; p. 6, Report on Business, November 1992; p. 7, Office of the Registrar General of Ontario, 1992

Primary concerns...
p. 7, Children's Hospitals Injury Reporting and Prevention Program, November 1993; p. 8, Toronto Star, February 28/93; p. 8, Toronto Star, May 15/93; p. 9, Toronto Star, May 10/93; p. 9, Canadian Social Trends, 1993; p. 9, Canadian Social Trends, 1993; p. 10, Ontario Medicine, July 1994; p. 10, Toronto Star, December 8/93; p. 10, Toronto Star, November 19/93

Child behaviour...
p. 11, Maclean's, January 2/95

Teen scene...
p. 11, Profiles, September 1993; p. 12, Globe and Mail, November 13/92; p. 12, Globe and Mail, October 7/94; p. 12, Toronto Star, September 23/93; p. 13, Toronto Star, March 4/95; p. 13, Toronto Star, May 14/93; p. 13, Toronto Star, February 12/94; p. 13, Toronto Star, March 9/94; p. 14, Sexual Assault—Pornography: The Links, a pamphlet by the Ontario Women's Directorate, 1992; p. 14, Maclean's, December 21/92; p. 14, Globe and Mail, June 25/93; p. 15, Toronto Star, June 7/94

Fun for all...
p. 15, Toys and Games, Vol. 19, No. 4, Sept. 1991; p. 15, Toys and Games, Vol. 19, No. 4, Sept. 1991; p. 16, Toys and Games, Vol. 19, No. 4, Sept. 1991; p. 16, Toys and Games, Vol. 19, No. 4, Sept. 1991; p. 16, Toys and Games, Vol. 19, No. 2, May 1991; p. 16, Toronto Star, April 2/94

Femme facts...

p. 17, Toronto Star, July 18/93; p. 17, Toronto Life, November 1992; p. 17, Toronto Life, November 1992; p. 17, Toronto Life, November 1992; p. 18, Toronto Life, November 1992; p. 18, Toronto Star, September 4/94; p. 18, Toronto Star, September 4/94; p. 18, Canadian Social Trends 1993; p. 19, Globe and Mail, May 8/93; p. 19, Chatelaine, November 1992

Womenspeak...

p. 19, Toronto Star, April 7/94; p. 20, Report on Business, July 1994; p. 20, Report on Business, December 1993; p. 20, Report on Business, December 1993; p. 21, Dating Around the World Survey by Harlequin Enterprises, February 1994; p. 21, Report on Business, November 1993

Looking for love?...

p. 22, Homemaker's, Jan./Feb. 1994

Buying beauty...

p. 22, Statistics Canada Catalogue 63-233; p. 23, Toronto Star, December 26/92

Seniority...

p. 23, Abilities, Spring 1992; p. 23, Canadian Business, July 1992; p. 24, Toronto Star, August 20/94

Mature money...

p. 24, Abilities, Spring 1992; p. 24, Abilities, Spring 1992

Elder care...

p. 24, Toronto Star, November 5/93; p. 25, Canadian Family Physician, October 1992; p. 25, Canadian Social Trends, 1993; p. 25, Canadian Social Trends, 1993

Parting words...

p. 26, Statistics Canada Catalogue 63-233, January 1994; p. 26, Toronto Star, May 9/94; p. 26, Canadian Living, November 1993; p. 27, Toronto Star, September 27/93; p. 27, Toronto Life, June 1993; p. 27, Globe and Mail, October 30/93

Doggie data...

p. 28, Toronto Star, February 6/94; p. 28, Toronto Star, January 16/93; p. 29, Ontario Veterinary Association, Toronto Star, May 22/93; p. 29, Globe and Mail, June 26/93

Pet ills, vet bills...

p. 30, Financial Times of Canada, April 30/94; p. 31, Canadian Living, November 1994

OUR BELIEFS

Religious affiliation...

p. 33, Canadian Social Trends, 1993

Let us sing...

pp. 33–34, Toronto Star, April 16/94

Sistering...

p. 34, Toronto Star, October 25/93; p. 35, Toronto Star, October 25/93

A significant synagogue...

p. 35, Toronto Life, December 1992

Zen...

p. 35, Toronto Star, July 10/93

SCHOOL DAYS

Educational achievement...

p. 37, Time, February 6/95

A primary glimpse...

p. 37, Profiles, September 1994; p. 38, Chatelaine, March 1994

Strictly private...

pp. 38–39, Financial Post Magazine, September 1993

A secondary look...

p. 39, Time, February 6/95; p. 40, Time, February 6/95; p. 40, Time, February 6/95; p. 40, Report on Business, November 1992; p. 41, Toronto Star, December 2/93; p. 41, Report on Business, November 1992; p. 41, Homemakers, April 1993; p. 41, Toronto Star, May 15/93

A higher degree...

p. 42, Toronto Star, September 23/93; p. 42, Statistics Canada Catalogue 81-219 Annual 1992; p. 42, Maclean's, August 15/94; p. 42, Toronto Star,

April 25/93; p. 43, Report on Business, August 1994; p. 43, Report on Business, August 1994; p. 43, Canadian Living, January 1994; p. 43, Globe and Mail, March 19/94

Student integrity...
p. 44, Maclean's, January 2/95; p. 44, Maclean's, January 2/95

Students from afar...
p. 45, Toronto Star, January 17/94; p. 45, Toronto Star, January 17/94

WORKING WAYS

Our financial position...
p. 47, Maclean's, January 2/95; p. 47, Maclean's, January 2/95

Incoming facts...
p. 48, Toronto Star, April 14/93; p. 48, Toronto Star, January 29/94; p. 48, Toronto Star, April 14/93; p. 49, Toronto Star, March 30/94; p. 49, Toronto Star, March 30/94; p. 49, Maclean's, August 15/94; pp. 50–51, Toronto Star, May 2/93; p. 51, Canadian Business, December 1992

Career moves...
p. 52, Maclean's, January 23/95; p. 52, Maclean's, January 23/95; p. 53, Homemakers, September 1993; p. 53, Time, February 6/95; p. 54, Toronto Star, July 17/93; p. 54, Time, February 6/95; p. 55, Maclean's, January 23/95

Danger pay...
p. 55, Toronto Star, December 14/92; p. 55, Toronto Star, November 21/92; p. 56, Toronto Star, November 21/92

In the workplace...
p. 57, Canadian Living, March 1994; p. 57, Canadian Living, March 1994; p. 57, Canadian Living, March 1994; p. 57, Toronto Star, January 22/94; p. 57, Maclean's, December 21/92; p. 58, Report on Business, February 1994; p. 58, Toronto Star, February 8/94; p. 58, Toronto Star, November 21/92; p. 59, Toronto Star, March 5/94; p. 59, Maclean's, October 1993; p. 59, Maclean's, January 2/95; p. 60, From Canada's Best Employers for Women: A Guide for Job Hunters, Employees and Employers by Tema Frank, Globe and Mail, January 14/95

CBC...
pp. 60–61, Globe and Mail, March 26/94

Creative employment...
p. 61, Globe and Mail, January 22/94

Domestic bliss?...
p. 62, Toronto Star, February 1/93

Thoughts of retirement...
p. 62, Canadian Social Trends 1993; p. 62, Financial Forum, February 1994

BETTER HOMES AND GARDENS

The state of real estate...
p. 64, Globe and Mail, January 28/95; pp. 64–65, Globe and Mail, January 1/93; p. 65, Toronto Star, May 12/93; p. 65, Toronto Star, May 12/93

From a woman's point of view...
p. 66, Chatelaine, April 1994; pp. 66–67, Chatelaine, April 1994

Togetherness...
p. 67, Maclean's, January 10/94

A growing concern...
p. 68, Toronto Star, August 21/94; p. 68, Toronto Star, August 21/94

NATIONAL HEALTH

Health care in Canada...
p. 70, Maclean's, January 2/95

The cost of health...
p. 71, Canadian Living, February 1993; p. 71, Canadian Family Physician, October 1992; p. 71, Toronto Star, February 8/93; p. 71, Toronto Star, January 9/93; p. 72, Homemakers, March 1994

Hospital zone...
p. 72, Report on Business, November 1993; p. 72, Toronto Star, April 19/93; p. 73, Canadian Living, August 1993

Under the knife...
p. 73, Toronto Star, July 3/93; p. 73, Globe and Mail, June 18/94; p. 73, Toronto Star, May 22/93; p. 74, Canadian Living, January 1993, Toronto Life, February 1994; p. 74, Toronto Star, October 19/93 and November 6/93; p. 74, Report on Business, October 1993

Operation prime time...
p. 75, Toronto Star, November 17/93

The ultimate gift...
p. 75, Canadian Social Trends, 1993; p. 75, Toronto Star, April 17/94; p. 76, Canadian Social Trends 1993; p. 76, Globe and Mail, April 2/93, Canadian Organ Replacement Register, 1992; p. 77, Globe and Mail, April 2/93; p. 77, Canadian Social Trends, 1993

Are you my type?...
p. 78, Toronto Star, April 25/93; pp. 78–79, Toronto Star, August 27/94; p. 79, Globe and Mail, April 30/94; p. 79, Toronto Star, February 15/94; p. 79, Toronto Star, June 2/93

Take a pill...
p. 80, Toronto Star, April 4/93; p. 80, Ontario Medicine, August 1994; p. 80, HealthWatch, Fall 1992; p. 81, Toronto Star, May 12/93; p. 81, Maclean's, February 7/94; p. 81, Maclean's, May 23/94; p. 81, Witness, CBC TV, July 27/93; p. 82, Globe and Mail, April 22/94; p. 82, Toronto Star, March 25/94; p. 82, Toronto Star, August 27/94; p. 83, Toronto Star, October 2/93

In the beginning...
p. 83, Chatelaine, October 1993; p. 84, Toronto Star, January 4/93; p. 84, Toronto Star, November 13/93; p. 84, Toronto Star, May 13/93, Toronto Star, April 28/93; p. 85, Chatelaine, August 1993

Disabling conditions...
p. 85, Homemakers, April 1993; p. 85, Canadian Living, August 1993; p. 86, Abilities, Fall 1993; p. 86, Toronto Star, May 13/94; p. 86, Canadian Social Trends, 1993; p. 86, HealthWatch, Fall 1992; p. 87, Canadian Living, May 1994; p. 87, Toronto Star, May 8/93; p. 87, Toronto Star, January 11/94

What's love got to do with it?...

p. 87, Globe and Mail, May 8/93; p. 88, Globe and Mail, March 26/94; p. 88, Toronto Star, July 11/93; p. 88, Toronto Star, May 24/94; pp. 88–89, Toronto Star, July 11/93; p. 89, Toronto Star, May 10/93; p. 89, Toronto Star, December 3/92; p. 89, Canadian Living, April 1994

Just a slight adjustment...

p. 90, Canadian Living, March 1994

Is it hot in here?...

p. 90, Toronto Star, February 23/95

Seeing food as the enemy...

p. 90, Chatelaine, September 1993; p. 91, Canadian Family Physician, January 1993; p. 91, Canadian Family Physician, January 1993; p. 91, Canadian Family Physician, January 1993

Substantial substance abuse...

p. 91, Toronto Star, November 5/93; p. 92, Ontario Medicine, February 1993

Remodelling ourselves...

p. 92, Maclean's, October 12/94; p. 93, Financial Times of Canada, May 28/94; p. 93, Toronto Star, December 1/93; p. 93, Toronto Star, December 1/93; p. 94, Toronto Star, December 1/93; p. 94, Toronto Star, December 1/93; p. 94, Toronto Star, December 1/93

Mr. Sandman...

p. 94, Today's Health, September 1993; p. 95, Report on Business, December 1993; p. 95, Report on Business, December 1993; p. 95, HealthWatch, Fall 1992

Bathroom matters...

p. 96, Canadian Family Physician, October 1992; p. 96, Toronto Star, April 2/94; p. 96, Financial Times of Canada, July 3/93; p. 97, Toronto Star, March 24/94; p. 97, HealthWatch, Spring 1993

Pass the odour eaters...

p. 97, Canadian Living, August 1993

CLAIMS TO FAME

The best country in the world...

p. 99, Toronto Star, May 28/94; p. 100, Toronto Star, May 16/93; p. 100, Maclean's, October 10/94; p. 101, Canadian Living, November 1994

Inventive Canadians...

p. 101, Toronto Life, November 1992; p. 101, Toronto Life, November 1992; p. 102, Toronto Star, January 10/94; p. 102, Toronto Star, September 16/93, Maclean's, December 20/93; p. 102, Toronto Star, January 10/94; p. 103, Toronto Star, July 2/93; p. 103, Toronto Life, November 1992

Made in Canada?...

p. 103, The North West Company, Winnipeg, March 14/95

The biggest and the busiest...

p. 104, Toronto Star, March 22/93; p. 104, Toronto Star, December 18/93; p. 104, Toronto Star, August 19/94; p. 104, Toronto Star, June 27/94; p. 105, Toronto Star, September 18/93; p. 105, Toronto Star, June 30/94; p. 105, Toronto Star, November 16/93; p. 106, Toronto Star, April 9/94; p. 106, Toronto Life, October 1994

Well established...

p. 106, Toronto Star, September 17/93; p. 107, Toronto Star, May 14/93; p. 107, Jordan Britnell, June 4/93

Uniquely ours...

p. 107, Maclean's, April 4/94

Tiptoe through the tulips...

p. 108, Maclean's, May 23/94

People of note...

p. 108, Ontario Medicine, November 1992; p. 109, Globe and Mail, May 29/93; p. 109, Toronto Star, June 9/93, Globe and Mail, March 3/95; p. 109, The National Enquirer, October 18/94

Companies of distinction...

p. 110, Toronto Star, January 28/94; p. 110, Toronto Star, April 29/93; p. 110, Toronto Star, December 24/93

Canadians who care...

p. 111, Toronto Star, May 12/94; p. 111, Toronto Life, December 1993; p. 111, Toronto Star, June 14/93; p. 112, Breakfast Television, CITY-TV, March 9/94; p. 112, Welcome Wagon Advertisement in the mail, April 1994

Incredible edibles...

p. 112, Canadian Grocer, January 1993; p. 113, Ontario Foodfare, Fall 1994; p. 113, Toronto Star, September 18/93; p. 114, Report on Business, November 1993; p. 114, Canadian Grocer, March 1993; p. 114, Toronto Life, November 1992; p. 115, Report on Business, April 1994; p. 115, Toronto Star, October 9/93; p. 115, Toronto Life, November 1992; p. 116, Toronto Star, June 5/94; p. 116, Toronto Star, October 22/93; p. 116, Toronto Life, June 1993

Land claims...

p. 117, Toronto Star, July 25/93; p. 117, Globe and Mail, June 12/93

The maple leaf forever...

p. 118, Toronto Star, May 10/93; p. 118, Toronto Star, February 15/93; p. 118, Toronto Star, February 15/93

The Dionnes...

p. 118, Toronto Star, July 9/93

Believe it or not...

p. 119, Globe and Mail, April 23/94; p. 119, Toronto Star, April 2/94; p. 120, Toronto Star, November 5/93; p. 120, Queen St. Mental Health Centre Newsletter, January 1994

California dreaming...

p. 120, Toronto Star, October 2/94

Notable neighbourhoods...

p. 121, Toronto Star, July 21/94

PROVINCIAL AFFAIRS

Parlez-vous français?...

p. 123, Toronto Star, March 9/93

Pacifically speaking...

p. 123, B.C. Trivia, 1992; p. 124, Toronto Star, December 7/92; p. 124,

Canadian Living, December 1/94; p. 124, B.C. Trivia, 1992; p. 125, Toronto Star, April 18/93; p. 125, B.C. Trivia, 1992; p. 125, B.C. Trivia, 1992; p. 125, B.C. Trivia, 1992; p. 126, B.C. Trivia, 1992; p. 126, B.C. Trivia, 1992; p. 126, B.C. Trivia, 1992; p. 126, B.C. Trivia, 1992; p. 127, B.C. Trivia, 1992; p. 127, B.C. Trivia, 1992; p. 127, B.C. Trivia, 1992

Prairie ponderings...

p. 127, Canadian Living, August 1993; p. 128, Canadian Living, December 1993, Maclean's, August 8/94; p. 128, Alberta Trivia, 1992; p. 129, Alberta Trivia, 1992; p. 129, Globe and Mail, July 16/94; p. 129, Alberta Trivia, 1992; p. 130, Canadian Living, August 1993; p. 130, Maclean's, August 8/94; p. 130, Toronto Star, September 18/93, Canadian Living, February 1995; p. 130, Canadian Living, November 1993; p. 131, The Weather Network, March 11/95

Ontario — yours to discover...

p. 131, Toronto Star, October 2/94; p. 131, Globe and Mail, April 23/94; p. 131, Toronto Life, August 1994; p. 132, Toronto Star, January 29/94; p. 132, Globe and Mail, September 16/94; p. 132, Toronto Star, March 23/94; pp. 132–33, Toronto Star, November 17/94

La belle province...

p. 133, Maclean's, January 23/95; p. 134, Report on Business, November 1993; p. 134, Maclean's, October 3/94; p. 134, Maclean's, October 3/94; p. 134, Report on Business, November 1993; p. 135, Report on Business, November 1993, Maclean's, October 3/94; p. 135, Report on Business, November 1993; p. 135, Maclean's, October 3/94; p. 135, Maclean's, October 3/94; p. 136, Report on Business, November 1993; p. 136, Report on Business, November 1993, Maclean's, October 3/94; p. 136, Canadian Living, August 1993; p. 137, Report on Business, November 1993; p. 137, Report on Business, November 1993; p. 137, Report on Business, November 1993; p. 137, Maclean's, October 3/94

Maritime musings...

p. 138, Toronto Star, May 15/94; p. 138, Toronto Star, June 22/94; p. 138, Toronto Star, May 15/94; p. 138, Report on Business, August 1994; p. 139, Globe and Mail, January 14/95; p. 139, Globe and Mail, August 24/94; p. 140, Maclean's, May 23/94; p. 140, Canadian Living, December 1994; p. 140, Canadian Living, December 1994; p. 140, Maclean's, January 23/95; p. 141, Maclean's, January 3/94; p. 141, Globe and Mail, January 2/93

THAT'S ENTERTAINMENT
Reel time...
p. 143, Toronto Star, January 31/93; p. 143, Toronto Star, February 18/94; p. 143, Toronto Star, February 18/94

Video views...
p. 144, Toronto Sun, November 30/93; p. 144, Globe and Mail, February 12/93

On the tube...
p. 145, Dear Answer Lady, by Marg Meikle; p. 145, Canadian Business, May 1992; p. 145, Ability Network, January 1994; p. 146, Toronto Star, March 30/94; p. 146, Toronto Star, January 24/93; p. 146, Homemakers, September 1992; p. 146, Globe and Mail, May 21/93

Have you heard?...
p. 147, Canadian Living, January 1994; p. 147, Globe and Mail, December 11/92; p. 147, Maclean's, November 8/93; p. 147, Toronto Star, November 7/94; p. 148, Maclean's, November 8/93; p. 148, Toronto Star, May 22/94; p. 148, Toronto Star, February 26/94; p. 148, Maclean's, November 8/93, Toronto Star, June 4/93; p. 149, Canadian Business, August 1992

Read this...
p. 149, Globe and Mail, April 30/93; p. 149, Toronto Star, June 25/94; p. 150, Toronto Star, January 14/93; p. 150, Maclean's, April 4/94; p. 150, Report on Business, November 1993; p. 151, Toronto Star, February 23/95; p. 151, Toronto Star, May 22/94; p. 151, Canadian Business, September 1992; p. 151, Toronto Star, July 12/94; p. 152, Toronto Star, February 18/95; p. 152, Maclean's, October 10/94; p. 152, Globe and Mail, February 18/95; p. 153, Toronto Star, February 6/93

Live on stage...
p. 153, Globe and Mail, November 14/92; p. 154, Toronto Star, April 20/93; p. 154, Globe and Mail, January 22/94; p. 154, Toronto Star, November 9/93

Do not pass Go, do not collect $200...
p. 154, Maclean's, December 20/93

Impressive numbers...
    p. 155, Globe and Mail, January 6/95

LET'S EAT!

The staff of life...
    p. 157, Toronto Star, February 24/93

Tea time...
    p. 157, Toronto Star, January 31/95

Something fishy...
    p. 157, Report on Business, May 1993

Fowl play...
    p. 158, Canadian Grocer, May 1993

Pass the pasta...
    p. 158, Toronto Life, November 1992

Cukiness...
    p. 158, Agriculture Canada 1993

A lot of fungi...
    p. 159, Canadian Grocer, May 1993

Honey, honey...
    p. 159, Canadian Honey Council, Canadian Living, February 1995

For our health...
    p. 160, Canadian Grocer, May 1993

Gourmet goodies...
    p. 160, Toronto Star, November 28/93; p. 160, Toronto Star, March 14/94

Something kosher...
    p. 161, Canadian Grocer, March 1993

Something sweet...
    p. 161, Statistics Canada Catalogue 32-026, 1992; p. 161, Toronto Star,
    December 7/93; p. 162, Toronto Star, August 18/94; p. 162, Report on
    Business, November 1992; p. 162, Report on Business, November 1992;

p. 162, Report on Business, November 1992; p. 162, Toronto Life, November 1992; p. 163, B.C. Trivia, 1992; p. 163, Toronto Star, September 18/93; p. 163, Canadian Grocer, June 1993; p. 164, Report on Business, October 1993

You can't eat only one...
p. 164, Eye on Toronto, May 31/93

Oh, I forgot my list...
p. 164, Toronto Star, October 13/94; p. 165, Canadian Grocer, November 1992; p. 165, Canadian Grocer, March 1993; pp. 165–66, Canadian Grocer, March 1993

In the kitchen cupboards of the nation...
pp. 166–67, Chatelaine, February 1994; p. 167, Kraft General Foods Survey, May 1993; p. 167, Toronto Star, November 7/93; p. 168, Canadian Grocer, January 1993

Sugar and spice...
p. 168, Toronto Star, July 2/93; pp. 168–69, Toronto Star, January 13/93

Recipes for success...
p. 169, Dave Nichol's Insider's Report, March 1994; p. 169, Dave Nichol's Insider's Report, March 1994

Wine, beer and spirits...
p. 170, Toronto Life's Epicure, December 1992; p. 170, Canadian Living, April 1995; p. 170, Toronto Star, May 11/94; p. 171, Toronto Star, May 17/94; p. 171, Toronto Star, October 8/94

Menu choices...
p. 171, Toronto Star, July 15/93

RECREATIONAL PURSUITS

Batter up...
p. 173, Toronto Star, January 2/93; p. 173, Toronto Star, April 1/93; p. 174, Toronto Star, November 5/92; p. 174, Maclean's, April 26/93; p. 174, Toronto Star, January 2/93; p. 175, Toronto Star, June 10/93; p. 175, Globe and Mail, May 8/93; p. 175, Toronto Star, November 7/93; p. 175, Toronto Life, May 1993

The puck stops here...
p. 176, Toronto Star, June 3/93; p. 176, Toronto Star, March 5/93; p. 176, Globe and Mail, November 21/92; p. 177, Globe and Mail, April 16/93; p. 177, Toronto Star, June 5/93; p. 177, Toronto Star, June 10/94; p. 178, Toronto Star, January 6/93; p. 178, Toronto Star, January 23/93; p. 178, Globe and Mail, January 16/93

Skating figures...
p. 178, Participaction Ad in the Journal of the Canadian Dental Association, April 1993; p. 179, Toronto Star, November 21/92; p. 179, Toronto Star, March 14/95

A bevy of bonspiels...
p. 179, Toronto Star, February 7/93; p. 179, Toronto Star, February 7/93

It's all downhill from here...
p. 180, Maclean's, March 21/94; p. 180, Report on Business, September 1994

A misnomer...
p. 180, Toronto Star, February 5/94

A touchy subject...
p. 181, Canadian Living, November 1993

Playing around...
p. 181, CTV News, January 22/95; p. 181, Report on Business, November 1992; p. 181, Financial Times, September 10/94; p. 182, Runzheimer International Survey, July 1993, Toronto Star, July 3/93; p. 182, Toronto Star, July 5/93

The horsey set...
p. 182, Globe and Mail, July 9/93; p. 183, Toronto Star, May 1/93

Pedal power...
p. 183, Maclean's, July 26/93; p. 183, Maclean's, July 26/93; p. 184, Maclean's, July 26/93; p. 184, Report on Business, September 1994

Riding the waves...
p. 184, Report on Business, September 1994; p. 184, Financial Times of Canada, July 17/93; p. 185, Toronto Star, July 3/93

Incentive travel...
p. 196, Destinations, Globe and Mail, May 1993; p. 196, Report on Business, January 1993, Toronto Star, October 4/94

On the road to...
p. 196–97, Globe and Mail, May 13/94

Commuting...
p. 197, Toronto Star, June 2/94; p. 198, Toronto Star, June 2/94

Wheel luxury...
p. 198, Toronto Star, March 13/94; p. 199, Toronto Star, January 13/94

Wheel sporty...
p. 199, Toronto Star, January 30/94; p. 199, Toronto Star, May 29/93

Changing hands...
p. 199, Globe and Mail, November 6/92; p. 200, Financial Times of Canada, February 25/95

Free wheeling...
p. 200, Globe and Mail, November 6/92

Now you see it...
p. 200, Toronto Star, January 26/95; p. 201, Toronto Star, January 26/95; p. 201, Toronto Star, March 4/95

Driving costs...
p. 202, Financial Post Magazine, July/August 1993

Under the hood...
p. 202, Castrol television advertisement, May 1993; pp. 202–203, Maclean's, January 2/95

Parking woes...
p. 203, Financial Times of Canada, February 25/95; p. 204, Toronto Star, May 8/94; p. 204, Toronto Star, May 8/94; p. 204, Toronto Star, March 26/94

Ride the rails...
p. 205, Canadian Living, November 1992

Water ways...
  p. 206, Toronto Star, July 24/94; p. 206, Toronto Star, July 25/93

Heading south...
  p. 206, Toronto Star, January 22/94; p. 207, Toronto Star, January 15/94;
  p. 207, Toronto Star, October 22/94

On the wild side...
  p. 207, CFTO News, May 21/93

A piece of the action...
  p. 207, Destinations, June 1993

Only in Canada...
  pp. 208–209, Toronto Star, November 22/94

CASHING IN

Cold hard cash...
  p. 211, Toronto Star, July 7/93; p. 211, Toronto Star, June 13/94; p. 211, Street
  Cents, CBC TV, May 2/93; p. 211, Toronto Star, January 7/93; p. 211, Toronto
  Star, May 21/94; p. 212, Toronto Star, June 13/94; p. 212, Toronto Star, March
  5/95; p. 212, Toronto Star, March 5/95; p. 213, Toronto Star, July 7/93; p. 213,
  Toronto Star, March 21/93

Forgotten funds...
  p. 213, Toronto Star, July 3/94

Stocking up...
  p. 214, Toronto Star, March 4/94; p. 214, Toronto Star, March 3/93

Taking credit...
  p. 214, Toronto Star, April 11/93; p. 215, CityPulse News, April 28/94; p. 215,
  Toronto Star, June 5/93; p. 215, Toronto Star, June 28/93; p. 216, Toronto
  Star, January 16/94

When credit's due...
  p. 216, Toronto Star, January 16/94

Charitable Canadians...

p. 217, Report on Business, November 1993; p. 217, Toronto Star, September 10/94; p. 217, Maclean's, August 15/94

You can't win without a ticket...

p. 217, Toronto Star, January 23/93; p. 218, Globe and Mail, October 23/93; p. 218, Globe and Mail, October 23/93; p. 218, Financial Post Magazine, September 1993; p. 219, Maclean's, January 9/95

Win, place or show?...

p. 219, Toronto Star, January 23/93; p. 219, Toronto Star, July 8/94

Under the "B"...

p. 220, Toronto Star, February 11/93; pp. 220–21, Globe and Mail, March 20/93

Casino Royale, Canadian style...

p. 221, Financial Times of Canada, September 24/94

What it costs...

p. 222, Globe and Mail, September 23/94; p. 222, Toronto Star, December 11/93; p. 223, Financial Times of Canada, May 7/94

Keeping up with the Joneses...

p. 223, Toronto Star, June 26/94; p. 224, Financial Times, May 14/94

Phantom pricing...

p. 225, Toronto Star, September 25/94

BUSINESS CONCERNS

Making it big...

p. 227, Toronto Star, May 18/94; p. 227, Toronto Star, March 15/94; p. 227, Toronto Star, December 2/93; p. 227, Toronto Star, April 5/94; p. 228, Toronto Star, May 18/94; p. 228, Maclean's, December 20/93; p. 228, Homemakers, September 1994

Hidden agendas...

p. 229, Homemakers, May 1994

It's all in the name...

p. 229, Toronto Star, March 23/94

Parcel post...
    pp. 238–39, Financial Post Magazine, December 1993; p. 239, Toronto Life,
    June 1993; p. 239, Toronto Star, February 12/94

You called?...
    p. 240, Toronto Star, February 22/94; p. 240, Toronto Star, November 20/94;
    p. 240, Globe and Mail, July 30/94; p. 240, Toronto Star, October 13/94

We've got your number...
    p. 241, Toronto Star, April 22/93

The hardware...
    p. 241, Maclean's, January 17/94; p. 241, Globe and Mail, May 22/93;
    pp. 241–42, Maclean's, January 2/95; p. 242, Maclean's, January 2/95;
    p. 242, Maclean's, January 2/95; p. 243, Toronto Star, March 17/94

The software...
    p. 243, Toronto Star, March 17/94; p. 244, Maclean's, January 2/95; p. 244,
    Canadian Living, February 1995

The information superhighway...
    p. 244, Toronto Star, March 6/94; p. 245, Maclean's, January 17/94; p. 245,
    Globe and Mail, December 24/94

Gizmos and gadgets...
    p. 245, Financial Times of Canada, April 16/94; p. 245, Report on Business,
    January 1994

Snap stats...
    p. 246, Toronto Star, November 1/93; p. 246, Globe and Mail, April 22/94

MARKETING COMMODITIES

All the best from Canada...
    p. 248, Maclean's, January 24/94; p. 248, Globe and Mail, July 9/94; p. 248,
    Macleans, October 10/94; p. 249, Toronto Star, January 17/94; p. 249,
    Canadian Living, April 1995; p. 249, Toronto Star, May 6/93; p. 249, Toronto
    Star, May 12/94; p. 250, Toronto Star, December 17/92; p. 250, Toronto Star,
    April 13/94; p. 250, Toronto Star, November 13/93; p. 250, Globe and Mail,
    July 3/93; p. 251, Toronto Star, March 5/94; p. 251, Toronto Star, March 5/94;
    p. 252, Toronto Star, March 5/94; p. 252, Dear Answer Lady, Marg Meikle

From abroad...
p. 253, Toronto Star, June 6/93; p. 253, Globe and Mail, April 2/93; p. 253, Report on Business, March 1995; p. 253, Toronto Star, January 23/93; p. 254, Globe and Mail, February 18/95; p. 254, Toronto Star, February 18/95; p. 254, Toronto Star, March 27/93

GOVERNING THOUGHTS
The debt...
p. 256, Canadian Business, May 1993

A taxing situation...
p. 256, Toronto Star, August 30/94, Toronto Star, January 29/94; p. 256, Financial Times of Canada Magazine, March 19–25/94; p. 257, Globe and Mail, May 1/93; p. 257, Financial Times of Canada Magazine, March 19–25/94; p. 257, Toronto Star, April 5/94; p. 258, Toronto Star, March 21/93; p. 258, Beer Connoisseur, Volume 1, Issue 1, May/June 1993

Parliamentary gems...
p. 258, Maclean's, January 24/94; p. 259, Toronto Star, May 30/93; p. 259, Toronto Star, February 16/93; p. 259, Maclean's, January 24/94; p. 260, Toronto Star, May 30/93

Women in the House...
pp. 260–61, Toronto Star, November 20/94

Social security...
p. 261, The Wealthy Banker's Wife: The Assault on Equality in Canada by Linda McQuaig, 1993; p. 261, Toronto Star, January 20/94

Money well spent?...
p. 262, Toronto Star, April 23/93

Inquiring minds want to know...
p. 263, Globe and Mail, July 3/93

Free trade...
p. 263, U.S. Department of Labor, Toronto Star, May 24/93

Our favourite topic...
p. 264, Toronto Star, March 23/94

Keeping the peace...

p. 264, Toronto Star, March 12/94; p. 264, Toronto Star, March 12/94; p. 264, Canadian Living, April 1995

CRIME AND PUNISHMENT

At risk...

p. 266, Maclean's, January 2/95; p. 266, Maclean's, January 2/95

Violent charges...

p. 267, Toronto Star, December 22/92; p. 267, Maclean's, January 2/95; p. 267, Maclean's, January 2/95

Armed and dangerous...

p. 268, Globe and Mail, April 15/94; p. 268, Toronto Star, June 11/94; p. 268, Globe and Mail, April 15/94; p. 268, Toronto Star, January 9/94; p. 269, Toronto Star, January 2/94; p. 269, Toronto Star, February 10/93

To serve and protect...

p. 269, Maclean's, January 2/95; p. 270, Maclean's, January 2/95; p. 270, Toronto Star, April 25/93; p. 270, Toronto Star, February 7/94; p. 271, Toronto Star, October 6/94

The case for DNA...

p. 271, Maclean's, February 6/95

Do the crime...

p. 272, Destinations, September 1993; p. 272, Toronto Star, April 14/94; p. 272, Toronto Star, March 3/93; p. 272, Toronto Star, March 23/93; p. 273, Toronto Star, May 31/93

Do the time...

p. 273, Canadian Business, October 1992; p. 273, Toronto Star, June 21/94; p. 274, Toronto Star, March 18/94

Leaving on a jet plane...

p. 274, Toronto Star, June 25/94; p. 274, Toronto Star, June 25/94

Silence is frozen...

p. 275, Toronto Star, March 5/95

OUR GREAT LAND

Abusing our country...
p. 277, Globe and Mail, January 2/93; p. 278, Toronto Star, December 14/92; p. 278, Toronto Star, March 23/93; p. 278, Maclean's, January 25/93; p. 278, Maclean's, January 9/95; p. 279, Financial Times, June 4/94; p. 279, Canadian Business, September 1992; p. 279, Toronto Star, April 18/93; p. 279, Canadian Packaging, November 1992

Waste not, want not...
p. 280, World Wildlife Fund, February 16/94; p. 280, Canadian Packaging, November 1992; p. 280, Toronto Star, April 22/93; p. 281, Canadian Packaging, November 1992

Tree-huggers...
p. 281, Canadian Social Trends 1993; p. 281, Canadian Packaging, November 1992; p. 282, Canadian Family Physician, January 1993; p. 282, Profiles, December 1992; p. 282, Canadian Packaging, November 1992; p. 282, B.C. Trivia, 1992; p. 283, B.C. Trivia, 1992; p. 283, B.C. Trivia, 1992; p. 283, Toronto Star, April 17/93; p. 284, B.C. Trivia, 1992; p. 284, Toronto Star, February 27/94

Giving to Greenpeace...
p. 284, Toronto Star, June 9/93

How cold was it?...
p. 285, Globe and Mail, March 13/95

CELEBRATIONS

Lighten Up Canada Day...
p. 287, Toronto Star, February 6/93; p. 287, Toronto Star, March 5/94

Will you be my Valentine?...
p. 288, Toronto Star, May 8/94; p. 288, Toronto Star, May 8/94; p. 288, Toronto Star, February 14/94; p. 288, Toronto Star, February 14/94

Coloured eggs and chocolate bunnies...
p. 289, Toronto Star, May 8/94; p. 289, Toronto Star, May 8/94; p. 289, Toronto Star, May 8/94

Just for Moms...
  p. 289, Toronto Star, May 8/94; p. 290, Toronto Star, May 8/94; p. 290,
  Toronto Star, May 8/94; p. 290, Toronto Star, May 8/94

A day for Dads...
  p. 290, Toronto Star, May 8/94; p. 291, Toronto Star, May 8/94; p. 291,
  Toronto Star, May 8/94

Thanks for giving...
  p. 291, Toronto Star, May 8/94

A day to remember...
  p. 291, CBC Remembrance Day Services, November 11/93; p. 292, Maclean's,
  October 10/94

Deck the halls...
  p. 292, Globe and Mail, December 11/92; p. 292, Globe and Mail, December
  11/92; p. 293, Homemakers, November/December 1992; p. 293, Toronto Star,
  May 8/94; p. 293, Alberta Trivia, 1992; p. 294, Toronto Star, May 8/94;
  p. 294, Toronto Star, May 8/94; p. 294, Toronto Star, December 24/93; p. 294,
  Homemakers, Nov./Dec. 1993; p. 295, Toronto Star, December 8/94; p. 296,
  Toronto Star, January 7/95

WHERE WE BELONG

Join the club...
  p. 298, Toronto Star, March 5/94; p. 298, Toronto Star, April 14/93; p. 298,
  Financial Times of Canada, March 5/94

Brain strain...
  p. 299, Toronto Star, November 14/92

Happy campers...
  p. 299, Maclean's, February 27/95

Swat team...
  p. 300, Toronto Star, July 13/93

Out of context...
  p. 300, Toronto Star, July 15/93

Relating and relationships...
p. 313, Homemakers, October 1993; p. 313, Toronto Star, July 19/93

An affair to remember...
pp. 313–14, Maclean's, January 2/95; pp. 314–15, Maclean's, January 2/95

Barbie loves Ken...
p. 315, Toys and Games, Vol. 20, No. 1, Jan./Feb. 1992

What a thought!...
p. 316, Homemakers, September 1994

Getting personal...
p. 316, Maclean's, January 3/94; pp. 316–17, Maclean's, January 3/94;
p. 317, Maclean's, January 3/94; p. 317, Maclean's, January 3/94; p. 318,
Maclean's, January 3/94

Let's talk about sex...
p. 318, Maclean's, January 3/94; p. 319, Maclean's, January 2/95; p. 319,
Maclean's, January 3/94; p. 319, Maclean's, January 3/94; p. 320, Maclean's,
January 2/95; p. 320, Maclean's, January 3/94; pp. 320–21, Maclean's,
January 2/95; p. 321, Homemaker's, September 1992

How we feel...
p. 321, Homemakers, April 1994; p. 322, Toronto Star, November 23/92

Hard at work...
p. 322, Toronto Star, June 7/93; p. 323, Homemakers, November/December
1993; p. 323, Report on Business, March 1995

Juicy trial...
p. 324, Globe and Mail, April 14/95

Would you lend your toothbrush?...
p. 324, Report on Business, January 1994;

Final thoughts...
pp. 324–25, Globe and Mail, September 9/94